MAKING MORE WORDS

Multilevel, Hands-on Phonics and Spelling Activities

by
Patricia M. Cunningham
and
Dorothy P. Hall

Good Apple

Dedication

This book is dedicated to Margaret Defee—the first-grade teacher who piloted the "4Blocks" at Clemmons Elementary and who not only understood "Making Words" but created many of the first lessons and became the model for other teachers who followed. Margaret is now the Curriculum Coordinator at Easton Elementary—a Title I school in Winston-Salem, North Carolina.

And a special thanks to the teachers and children of Clemmons, Cash, and Easton Elementary Schools in Winston-Salem, North Carolina, who have been "Making Words" for years and who we have been watching and from whom we have learned.

Designers
Ruth Otey
Deborah Walkoczy

Cover
Peter Van Rysen
Bernadette Hruby
Lisa Arcuri

Editors
Susan Eddy
Donna Garzinsky

GOOD APPLE
A Division of Frank Schaffer Publications
23740 Hawthorne Blvd.
Torrance, CA 60505

ISBN 1-56417-900-1

5 6 7 8 9 MAL 01 00 99 98

CONTENTS

INTRODUCTION

Making More Words is an exciting and successful sequel to *Making Words*. It has been used by primary teachers who've chosen and adapted the lessons to suit the needs of their classes. The 140 lessons in *Making More Words* are arranged alphabetically by the final word that ends the lesson but can be used in any order (see the Lessons Index, on p. 22). The Patterns Index, on page 187, indicates the letter patterns that are sorted for in each lesson. This may be helpful if you wish to focus on a particular pattern to provide students extra practice.

In addition to the lessons and the indexes, *Making More Words* provides ten warm-up lessons to use as desired with your class (see p. 37), a section on the theory and research behind *Making More Words* (see p. 8), thematic tie-ins for cross-curricular use (see Curriculum Connections, p. 19), reproducible letter cards (p. 198), a sample letter to send home to families (p. 196), and take-home sheets (p. 197).

Making More Words is a manipulative, multilevel activity that both teachers and students enjoy. As children make and sort words, they increase their word knowledge, discover patterns, and become better readers and writers. If you ask the children what they think of *Making More Words* activities, they will probably answer, "They're fun!" From the moment that students get their letters, they begin moving the letters around and making whatever words they can. They are particularly eager to figure out the word that can be made with all the letters. Once the children begin making the words you've selected, the activity is fast-paced and keeps the children involved. The children also enjoy sorting the words. Finding words that rhyme, words that begin with the same letter or sound, words that can all be changed into other words by just moving around the letters, and other patterns is like solving a riddle or a puzzle. Invite your students on this enjoyable educational journey!

MORE ABOUT THIS BOOK

Making More Words contains ten warm-up lessons. Many teachers will use several warm-up lessons that contain only one vowel to help students meet immediate success and learn how to manipulate the letters to make words. Once children understand how to make words, the lessons will usually contain two vowels. Eventually, the number of vowels is unlimited.

Once you have introduced how to make words, choose or create lessons with words that can be integrated with your curriculum or that teach letter-sound patterns you wish children to focus on.

Each *Making More Words* lesson is multilevel in two ways. First, students begin by making simple, short words and then move on to making more complex, long words. Second, the word sorting is multilevel in that students sort for consonants, prefixes, suffixes, endings, blends, digraphs, rhymes, chunks, phonograms, and homophones. Since most classrooms contain students at all different stages of spelling/decoding ability, making easier and more difficult words and sorting for easier and more difficult patterns allow all students to increase their word knowledge.

Most lessons can be done in 15–20 minutes, with approximately two-thirds of the time spent making 10–15 words. The other one-third of the time is spent sorting words for patterns and transferring this word knowledge to spelling a few new words. Some lessons are so rich in possibilities for word making and pattern sorting that you may wish to designate them as two-day lessons. Or if a lesson seems too long, omit certain words and/or patterns. If you don't have enough time to do word sorting, choose fewer words for the next lesson. To keep the lesson multilevel, include words and patterns on a variety of levels. Some teachers worry that the least able students will not be able to make the long words and that the advanced students do not need to make the short words. Observations indicate that if the lessons are fast paced, most students stay involved. Even if some students don't get every letter of a word in place before the word is placed in the pocket chart, they usually get some of the letters and then finish the word by matching to the model. Advanced students enjoy making the short words and are eager to figure out what word can be made with all the letters.

To create letter cards for classroom use, duplicate the letter pages (pp. 199–204) on tagboard or index cards, using one color paper for the vowels and a different color paper for the consonants. (Some teachers prefer to make handwritten letter cards, using red markers for the vowels and black markers for the consonants.) Cut the letter cards apart and store in plastic zipper bags. See Distributing Letters, on page 17, for suggestions on how to distribute the letter cards for each lesson.

A slash (/) is used in some lessons to indicate that the next word in the list can be made by changing the order of the letters. Words with an asterisk (*) are harder to spell and may be omitted to make the lesson easier or shorter. Remember to include some harder words to make your lesson multilevel.

You may wish to give children copies of a completed take-home sheet (p. 197) to make words at home with their families. Write in the letters for a specific lesson on the take-home sheet and then duplicate the sheet for each student. Students can't wait to take the letter-sheets home and say, "I bet you don't know the word that can be made when you use all these letters!" At home they cut the letters out and let someone—parent, brother, sister, grandmother—try to make the word. They then proudly demonstrate words they can remember making and how they sorted these words into patterns.

A *Making More Words* activity is one in which children use letters to make words, beginning with two-letter words and continuing with three-, four-, and five-letter words and even bigger words until the final word is made. The final word always includes all the letters that students have that day. Children are usually eager to figure out what word can be made from all the letters. (Many teachers call this word the secret word or the mystery word.) Once the secret word is made, children close up the letters in their holders and sort the words into patterns, including beginning letters, endings, and rhyming words. These sorted words are then used to read and spell other rhyming words. Children discover letter-sound relationships and learn how to look for patterns in words as they make and sort words. They also learn that changing just one letter or the order of the letters changes the whole word (Cunningham & Cunningham, 1992).

For the first *Making More Words* lessons, we suggest using five-letter words that contain one vowel. Provide children with the five letters needed. (Note: It is recommended that the vowel letter be written in red or a color different from that of the consonants.) Inform the children that they have to use the vowel for every word. In the beginning lessons, emphasize the letter names and sounds and only make words in which you can hear all the letters when you stretch them out. Children learn how words change as different letters are added and they begin to understand the importance of where letters occur in the words. Once children have had some practice making words with just one vowel, teach lessons that have two or more vowels. In these lessons, contrast the sound of the vowels by the order in which the words are made. After children make the word *nut*, for example, have them change just the vowel to make the word *net*.

Making More Words is a multilevel activity because, within one instructional format, there are endless possibilities for discovering how our alphabetic system works. By beginning every *Making More Words* activity with some short, easy words and ending with a big word that uses all the letters, the lessons provide practice for the struggling learners and challenge for all. Children who lack phonemic awareness develop that awareness as they listen for the sounds in words in order to make the words and participate in the sorting for patterns. Children who have phonemic awareness learn letter-sound correspondences and spelling patterns. Through the sorting and transferring activities that conclude each lesson, children learn how they can use words they know to read and spell other words.

Spelling-pattern and word-family instruction has a long history in American reading instruction. Currently, research is converging from several areas that supports the long-standing practice of word family/ phonogram/spelling pattern instruction. The research of Treiman (1985) suggests that both children and adults find it much easier to divide syllables into their onsets (all letters before the vowel) and rimes (the vowel and what follows) than into any other units. Thus *Sam* is more easily divided into *S - am* than into *Sa - m* or *S - a - m*. It is easier and quicker for people to change *Sam* to *ham* and *jam* than it is to change *Sam* to *sat* and *sad*. In fact, Treiman concludes that the division of words into onsets and rimes is a "psychological reality." Wylie and Durrell (1970) listed 37 phonograms that could be found in almost 500 primary-grade words. These high-utility phonograms are

> *ack; ail; ain; ake; ale; ame; an; ank; ap; ash; at; ate; aw; ay; eat; ell; est; ice; ick; ide; ight; ill; in; ine; ing; ink; ip; it; ock; oke; op; ore; ot; uck; ug; ump; unk.*

Another area of research supporting spelling patterns is that conducted on decoding by analogy (Goswami & Bryant, 1990). This research suggests that once children have some words that they can read and spell, they use these known words to figure out unknown words. A reader confronting the infrequent word *mace* for the first time might access the known words *ace* and *race* and then use these words to generate a probable pronunciation for *mace.*

Brain research provides a different sort of support for word family instruction. Current theory suggests that the brain is a pattern detector, not a rule applier, and that decoding a word occurs when the brain recognizes a familiar spelling pattern or, if the pattern itself is not familiar, searches through its store of words with similar patterns (Adams, 1990). To decode the unfamiliar word *knob*, for example, the child who knew many words that began with *kn* would immediately assign to the *kn* the "n" sound. The initial *kn* would be stored in the brain as a spelling pattern. If the child only knew a few other words with *kn* and hadn't read these words very often, that child would probably not have *kn* as a known spelling pattern and thus would have to do a quick search for known words that began with *kn*. If the child found the words *know* and *knew* and then tried this same sound on the unknown word *knob*, that child would have used the analogy strategy. Likewise, the child might know the pronunciation for *ob* because of having correctly read so many words containing the *ob* spelling pattern or might have had to access some words with *ob* to use them to come up with the pronunciation. The child who had no stored spelling patterns for *kn* or *ob* and no known words to access and compare to would be unlikely to successfully pronounce the unknown word *knob*.

The understanding that the brain is a pattern detector explains a great deal about the popularity of word family/phonogram/spelling pattern instruction since, in one-syllable words, the vowel and following letters constitute the pattern that is most helpful in decoding. Realizing that the brain functions as a pattern detector also explains why successful reading does not require that all the patterns be taught. The patterns exist in the words, and children who know that the patterns exist and who read widely will discover the patterns. Henderson (1990) suggests that word sorting is a powerful activity for developing children's spelling abilities.

■ References ■

Adams, M. J. *Beginning to Read: Thinking and Learning About Print.* MIT Press, Cambridge, MA, 1990.

Cunningham, P. M. *Phonics They Use: Words for Reading and Writing* (2nd ed.). HarperCollins, New York, 1991.

Cunningham, P. M. and J. W. Cunningham. "Making Words: Enhancing the Invented Spelling-Decoding Connection." *The Reading Teacher,* 46, 106–115, 1992.

Goswami, U. and P. Bryant. *Phonological Skills and Learning to Read.* Erlbaum Associates, East Sussex, U.K., 1990.

Henderson, E. H. *Teaching Spelling* (2nd ed.). Houghton Mifflin, Boston, 1990.

Treiman, R. "Onsets and Rimes as Units of Spoken Syllables: Evidence From Children." *Journal of Experimental Child Psychology,* 39, 161–181, 1985.

Wylie, R. E. and D. D. Durrell. "Teaching Vowels Through Phonograms." *Elementary English,* 47, 787–791, 1970.

Preparing the Lesson

The teacher has decided that *stamp* is the word that will end the lesson. She has pulled out the large letter cards for *stamp*. Here, she is brainstorming lots of little words that can be made from the letters in *stamp*.

The teacher has decided which of the many words that could be made will make for an easy and successful first lesson. She writes these words on large index cards.

She puts these index cards in a small brown envelope. On the outside of the envelope, she writes the words in the order in which the children will make them, the patterns she will have the children sort for, and the transfer words.

Teaching the Lesson

The children are ready to make words. Their letters are placed in front of their holders (see p. 17 for holder construction tips).

The teacher holds up and names each large letter in the pocket chart. The children hold up and name the matching letters on their cards. The teacher writes a 2 on the board and says,
> "The first word I want you to make has just two letters—the vowel *a* plus one more. Everyone say *am*. I *am* your teacher. Find a letter to add to the *a* to spell *am*."

A child who has made *am* correctly comes to the pocket chart and makes the word by using the pocket-chart letters.
> "Good, *a-m* spells *am*. Everyone check *am* in your folder, and we are ready to make another word."

The teacher places the index card with the word *am* written on it in the pocket chart. She has the children change the last letter and spell the word *at*.
> "We are *at* school. Everyone say *at*. Stretch out the end of *at* and try to hear the letter that makes the sound at the end."

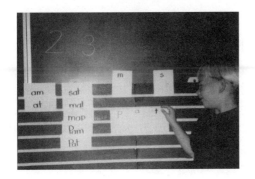

The teacher writes a 3 on the board and has them hold up 3 fingers. She tells the children to leave the word *at* in their holders and add just one letter at the beginning to change *at* to *sat*. She finds someone who has made the word correctly and asks him or her to come to the chart and make the word by using the big letters.

The teacher and children continue to make three-letter words.
"Now, take out the *s* and put in another letter, and you can change your *sat* to *mat*. Everyone say *mat*. In kindergarten you rested on your *mat*."

For each word a child who has made the word correctly comes and makes it with the big letters. The teacher places the index card for that word in the pocket chart. Each child checks or fixes his or her word before the teacher tells the next word.
"This time we are going to change the end of the word. Change the last letter and you can spell *map*. Everyone say *map*. We use a *map* when we go on trips."

"The next word is a person's name. The name is *Pam*. You can make *Pam* with the same three letters you have in your holder already for *map*, but you will have to put the letters in different places and begin the word with a capital letter."

"Now we are going to make another name. Leave your capital *P* and the *a* but take away the *m* and add a letter to spell the name *Pat*. Everyone say *Pat*."

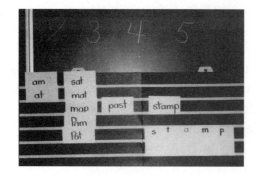

The teacher writes a 4 on the board.

"Now we are going to make a four-letter word. Add a letter to *pat* and spell *past*. Everyone say *past* slowly with me. Try to hear where you can add a letter to make *pat* into *past*."

The teacher tells the children that every *Making More Words* lesson ends with a word that uses all the letters.

"Move your letters around and see if you can make a word that uses all the letters."

She gives the children a minute to see if anyone can come up with the word. If a child does, that student comes to the pocket chart to make the word. If no one can, the teacher tells the children that the word is *stamp* and has them make it.

The teacher and children are now going to sort the words for patterns. The teacher takes the word *mat* and asks,

"Who can go find another word that begins with the letter *m*?"

A child goes to the pocket chart and places *map* under *mat*. The teacher and children pronounce *mat* and *map* and decide that they begin with the same letter and sound. The same procedure is used for *Pam*, *past*, and *Pat* and then *sat* and *stamp*.

Next the teacher goes to the pocket chart and pulls out the word *sat*.

"Now I need someone who can find two words that end in the letters *a-t*."

A child places *at*, *mat*, and *Pat* under *sat*. Teacher and children pronounce the words and decide that they all end in *at* and they all rhyme. The same procedure is followed with *am* and *Pam*.

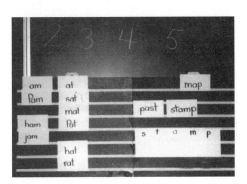

When *at, sat, mat,* and *Pat* are lined up under one another alongside *am* and *Pam*, the teacher says,

"When you are reading, you will see lots of words that end in *a-t* or *a-m*, and you can figure them out on your own if you think about how words with the same vowel and ending letter usually rhyme. What if you were reading and came to these words?"

The teacher writes the words *jam* and *rat* on index cards without pronouncing them. The children put these words under the rhyming words and then use the rhyming words to figure them out.

"Thinking of a rhyming word can help you when you are writing, too. What if you were writing and needed to figure out how to spell *ham* or *hat*?"

The children decide that *ham* rhymes with *am* and *Pam*. The word *ham* is written on an index card and placed under *am* and *Pam*. *Hat* is spelled and placed under *at, mat, sat,* and *Pat*.

▪ Tips for Successful Lessons ▪

These are some tips that many teachers have found helpful.

1. Pace your lesson quickly. If a lesson moves too slowly, children get bored! Don't wait for all students to make each word before sending someone to the pocket chart.

2. Adapt the lesson to your class. Leave out words that are too difficult for everyone or that the children have never heard of.

3. Have children say each word—not just listen for the word—before making it. They need to hear themselves making the sounds if they are going to transfer this ability to spelling words as they write.

4. Be sure to leave time to sort and transfer. Some children need to be explicitly taught how making words helps them read and spell. If the lesson's pace has been brisk and yet you run out of time to sort and transfer, make fewer words.

5. Remember that *Making More Words* is a multilevel activity. Send your strugglers to the pocket chart to make the easier words and your word wizards to make the more complex words.

6. Give children more guidance in making and sorting words early on in the year, then phase out some of that guidance. For example, early in the year you might say

   "Change the first letter to change *sat* to *mat.*"

   Later on say

   "Change just one letter to change *sat* to *mat.*"

   When sorting early in the year, say

   "Who can find the words that rhyme with *at?*"

   Later on say

   "Who can come and sort out the rhyming words?"

7. Consider giving children a take-home sheet for homework after doing the lesson in class. Write the letters on the sheet in alphabetical order, vowels then consonants so as not to give away the secret word. Duplicate and hand out. Children love knowing the secret word and stumping their parents!

8. Many primary teacher workrooms have a communal box filled with brown *Making More Words* envelopes. When a lesson is finished, it is added to the box for others to use.

9. Most lessons are used only once, but sometimes teachers use the same lesson again several months later, when it fits in with something else they are doing.

You may wish to provide holders for students to use.
Holders can be easily fashioned from file folders, using the
following directions.

- Cut several file folders into thirds vertically (approximately
  4 inches, or 10 cm, for each third), leaving the fold in the
  middle of each section. (You may find it easier to cut the
  folders by opening them out first.)

- Fold up the bottom, or long edge, of each section to create
  a pocket. Determine the pocket's depth by measuring the
  space under the letters on your letter cards.

- Crease the fold well and staple it just on the two ends to
  secure the pocket.

▪ Distributing Letters ▪

Develop a procedure for distributing the *Making More Words*
letters to students. Some suggestions that have worked for other
teachers include the following.

- Choose children to pass out the letters needed for a lesson.
  Select as many children as there are letters and give each
  one consonant or vowel to hand out to everyone. The same
  children pick up the letters at the end of the lesson.

- Put the letters needed for the lesson on trays or plates. As
  students come in in the morning and get ready for the day,
  have each child stuff a holder by picking up the letters,
  cafeteria style.

- Provide each child with a bag containing all the letters. Write
  the needed letters on the chalkboard and, before school or
  class starts, have children find their letters and put them in
  their holders.

▪ Planning Your Own Lessons ▪

Once you get started *Making More Words*, you will find the need to create lessons for words that tie into your content but that are not included in this book. It's fun and easy to plan lessons of your own. These are the steps we used to plan our lessons.

1. Decide what the final word in the lesson will be. In choosing this word, consider its number of vowels, student interest, what curriculum tie-ins you can make, and what letter-sound patterns you can draw children's attention to through the word sorting at the end of the lesson.

2. Make a list of shorter words that can be made from the letters of the final word.

3. From all the words you listed, pick approximately 10–15 words that include the following.

    a. Words that you can sort for the pattern(s) you want to emphasize

    b. Little words and big words so that the lesson is multilevel

    c. Words that can be made with the same letters in different places (*barn/bran*) so that students are reminded that when spelling words, the order of the letters is crucial

    d. A name or two to remind children where capital letters are used

    e. Words that most of the students have in their listening vocabularies

4. Write all the words on index cards and order them from smallest to biggest.

5. Once you have all the words together, sort them further so that you can emphasize letter patterns and how changing the position of the letters or changing/adding just one letter results in a different word.

6. Store the cards in an envelope. Write the words (in the order used) and patterns (sorted for at the end of the lesson) on the envelope.

To be effective, phonics and spelling instruction should be tied as closely as possible to what children are reading and learning about. In selecting the words that end the lessons in *Making More Words*, we have included many words that teachers use as part of their themes or units. Words with a number following them, such as "frogs (#7)," indicate warm-up lesson words.

Seasons
- acorns
- autumn
- leaves
- seasons
- spring
- summer

Weather
- forecast
- overcast
- puddles
- rainbow
- rainfall
- sleigh
- snowball
- snowman
- snowy
- sprinkle
- stormy
- sunlight
- sunshine
- umbrella
- weather

Celebration, Holiday Words
- birthday
- claps (#1)
- clowns
- Dancer
- Dasher
- decorate
- ghosts
- holidays
- Indians
- ornament
- parties
- Pilgrims
- piñata
- Prancer
- presents
- Ruldolph
- valentine

Math Words
- adding
- counting
- geometry
- graphing
- hundreds
- longest
- measure
- patterns
- practice
- shapes
- sorting
- subtract

Reading, Children's Books
- alphabet
- artists
- author
- (Big) Anthony
- castle
- Clifford
- Corduroy
- detective
- dinosaur
- dragons
- fiction
- friendly
- giants
- horrible
- journal
- kingdom
- Madeline
- painter
- prince
- Ramona
- rewards
- stories
- terrible

Animals
- beavers
- bunnies
- chicken
- duckling
- frogs (#7)
- kangaroo
- mammals
- penguins
- puppies
- raccoon
- reptiles
- turkeys
- whales

Health, Nutrition, Food
- fingers
- fruits
- grapes
- heart

19

macaroni
orange
pasta
playing
pretzels
slept
tacos
zucchini

Home, Family, Clothes
bathroom
bedroom
buttons
curtain
family
jackets
letters
manners
quilts
table
whisper

Science, Environment
camping
discover
Earth
electric
escape
feeders
flames
gardens
glowing
growing
hunts (#10)
knocking
machines
magnetic
matter
nature
nuclear
planting
pulleys
recycle

science
seedling
smelling
sprout
stung (#9)
watering

Sports, Music
cheering
contest
crowds
guitars
sport (#8)

Transportation
airplane
railroad
trucks

WARM-UP LESSONS INDEX

LESSONS INDEX

11. **bedroom** *b d r ed oom ore bled sled*   57
zoom store
do bed red rod rob rode robe room doom door
more bore bored broom rodeo bedroom

12. **birthday** *b h r br id ay aid skit stay card paid*   58
at it bit bid hid day ray bird bath hard yard
raid braid birth dairy*/diary* birthday

13. **bunnies** *b s in us ub win spin cub Gus*   59
in us bus bin sun sub buns bins nine
snub bunnies

14. **buttons** *b us ut out cut strut pout shout*   60
us bus but nut out bout bust nuts/stun stunt
stout snout bonus button buttons

15. **camping** *c m ing* (ending) *an ap ain plan*   61
trap snap gaining
am an can cap nap/pan man map camp
main pain gain magic manic panic pacing
camping

16. **castle** *c s sc s* (plural) *at et eat* ale jet vet*   62
beat scales*
at cat sat set let eat* seat* scat/cats/cast sale
tale tales/stale/steal* scale castle

17. **cheering** *h r ch ice dice twice spice*   63
in he hen her ice rice nice ring rich inch
here cheer hinge green nicer enrich cheering

18. **chicken** *h k n en in eck ick when slick*   64
peck then
in hi he hen Ken kin hick nick neck chick
check chicken

19. **Clifford** *c f old oil ord* (Names) *sold scold*   65
spoil lord
or if off for fir old oil foil coil cord cold
fold Ford cliff Clifford

20. **clowns** *c cl ow* (two pronunciations) *own* (two   66
pronunciations) *blow how show shown*
on cow owl/low now/own sown/nows slow/owls
cows clown scowl clowns

21. contest *c* (two pronunciations) *n* *s* (plural) *ent*
est ot spot vest spent crest
no to tot cot not one cone cost cent sent
ones nest test note notes cones cents contest 67

22. Corduroy *c r y od oy sod clod fly toy*
do or rod cod coy Roy dry cry door/odor
cord Corduroy 68

23. counting *c t ing* (ending) *ot rot slot*
going cutting
in to got cot cut out into unit coin* count
tonic* tunic* union* tuning toning* outing counting 69

24. crowds *c cr r w s* (plural) *od*
ow (two pronunciations)
do so sod cod rod row cow cows rows crow
cord word words/sword crowd crows cords crowds 70

25. curtain *c r t un ut ain* (two pronunciations)
shut Stan main plain
in an can tan ran run rut cut car cart runt/
turn tuna rain train curtain 71

26. Dancer *r c d ed* (ending) *an ear van plan*
spear speared
an Ed red ran can car end/den ear dear
near cane* card care cared/raced dance* Dancer 72

27. Dasher *h r sh ad ash ear herd-heard glad*
cash trash clear
as has had sad her ear hear herd rash dash
read reads hears heard share shared/Dasher 73

28. decorate *c d ear ate deer-dear fear smear*
gate plate
or at cat ate/eat ear dear deer date rate card
care crate eater create created decorate 74

29. detective *d t de* ie ice tied/tide lie nice*
*twice defer**
it tie die ice rice dice diet*/tide*/tied*/edit*
detect devise* deceive* detective 75

30. dinosaur *s r un oar* our* ound gun*
stun boar found 76

is in on or* our* son sun run sir air* oar*
soar* sour* rain ruin* iron* irons* radio* round
sound around dinosaur

31. **discover** *s d dr s* (plural) *ice ive nice spice* 77
live hives
is ice sir side/dies disc dice dive drive/diver
dives drove disco* cover* covers* drives/
divers discover

32. **dragons** *s r dr ag ang and bag snag* 78
bang brand
an and ran rag sag nag sang drag rang sang
sand grand drags dragon dragons

33. **duckling** *d l cl in id ing ink uck stuck sting* 79
spin slid
in kin/ink lid dig dug duck luck lick king
cling clink ducking duckling

34. **Earth** *h r ate eat gate plate seat treat* 80
he at hat rat/art eat/ate hate/heat
rate Earth

35. **electric** *l t ie it ice die knit vice twice* 81
it lit let tie lie ice rice lice tile tire* tree
tier* liter* elect erect* electric

36. **escape** *s p ea ape ace see-sea flea tape* 82
lace trace
as see sea pea/ape ace cap cape/pace peas/
apes space/capes escape

37. **family** *f m y ail ay spy try trail stay* 83
am if my fly Fay may/yam aim ail mail fail
film filmy family

38. **feeders** *f s s* (plural) *er* (ending) *ed ee fled* 84
flee fees sender
Ed red fed fee see seed deer feed free frees
feeds feeder seeder feeders

39. **fiction** *c f t in ot* (compound word) *shin skin* 85
spot shot
if in fin fit not cot not/ton tin into info font
coin tonic fiction

40. **fingers** *f s gr s* (plural) *in ir ing twin stir*   86
sting swings
is in fin fig fir sir fine* fire* grin/ring
sing/sign* fines* fires*/fries* rings/grins finger
singer fingers

41. **flames** *c s fl s* (plural) *ea eal ame*   87
elf tea squeal game shelf
am Sam sea elf flea self seal seam meal/lame
same fame flame fleas flames

42. **forecast** *f ate eat gate slate neat treat*   88
as at of for far fat eat/ate ear fear feat fast
cast star rate crate coast* force forces forest*
faster forecast

43. **friendly** *f fl fr ly* ed* (ending) *end* in ine*   89
kin spin dined twine
if in fin fir* fly fry dry red end* lend* line
fine find fire file* filed* fined* fired/fried field*
finder* finely* friend friendly

44. **fruits** *f s s* (plural) *st it ir urf kit skit post*   90
Smurfs
is it fit fir fur furs firs fits/fist/sift surf turf rust
fruit first fruits

45. **gardens** *r g gr s* (plural) *er* (ending) *ear ag fear*   91
flag grades ears
an ran rag age gas* ear gear dear aged rage
rags drag rang* range*/anger* grand grade
garden/danger* ranges* gardens

46. **geometry** *g m t tr oy erm eet* (Names) *boy*   92
perm tweet sweet
me go to get met Tom Roy toy try Troy
tree term germ meet greet meter
meteor* geometry

47. **ghosts** *g h s* (plural) *ot ost trot plot post posts*   93
so go got hot hog hogs/gosh shot/host
hosts/shots ghost ghosts

48. **giants** *t g s s* (plural) *in it ag ain skit*   94
wag brain stains
it in an ant/tan tin sit sat sag snag/sang
sing/sign* gain gains giant stain/saint*/satin* giants

49. **glowing** *g gl l w ing* (plural) *in ow*   95
(two sounds) *fin shin snow snowing*
in win wig log low/owl own glow long lion
wing going owning glowing

50. **grapes** *g r p s* (plural) *ap age nap snap*   96
cage stage
as gas gap sap rap rag rags rage page
gaps/gasp* grape/pager pages grasp* grapes

51. **graphing** *p r g gr ing* (ending) *in ap ain*   97
trap stain slap skin
in pin pig gap rap ran rain pain gain
grin grip* grain graph* aging paging graphing

52. **growing** *w r g gr ing* (ending) *in ing ow*   98
ring-wring twin spin slow swing*
on in win won/own row grow grin/ring wing
gown* grown* going wring* rowing growing

53. **guitars** *r t st s* (plural) *at ug it ar scat jug*   99
smug skit
it at sat rat/tar rag rug tug grit stir star
stair grits stairs guitar guitars

54. **Harold** *h l ad old oad mad sold scold toad*   100
or rod old oar had lad lord load road hold
hard hoard Harold

55. **heart** *h r at eat ear ate beat plate skate smear* 101
at he her the are ate/eat ear rat hat hate
rate/tear hear heat heart

56. **holidays** *h l d y ay old ash stay gold*   102
rash crash
he is his has/ash had hay lay old hold sold
load dash lash lady daily daisy shady
holiday holidays

57. **horrible** *h r b ole* oil mole stole foil spoil*   103
he or rob rib oil hoe* her hero* hole role*
robe* boil broil broiler horrible

58. **hundreds** *h r ed en end fed fled when spend*   104
he us Ed red end/den hen her herd send
rush under udder* rushed shudder* hundred
hundreds

59. Indians *s s* (plural) *an and in-inn van*   105
plan land stand
as an in inn and/Dan sad/ads aid said sand
inns Indian Indians

60. jackets *c j s st* s* (plural) *ake ack ask flake*   106
snack smack mask
as at cat/act ask task cats/cast cake take
sake sack jack jacks stack stake*/steak*
cakes jacket casket* jackets

61. journal *l r an on or* (Names) *plan for*   107
Don van
or on an Jan ran run nor/Ron oar our oral*
loan lunar* journal

62. kangaroo *r an ag on wag upon tag plan*   108
an or on Ron ran rag nag rang rank okra
groan/organ kangaroo

63. kingdom *k d in ind ing win sing swing find*   109
on in kin/ink dog dig kid kind king ding
mind oink doing kingdom

64. knocking *k kn in ink ick in-inn twin*   110
link drink flick
in go no/on non inn ink/kin kink king kick
Nick coin* oink* knock knocking

65. leaves *s l s* (plural) *ave ee see-sea*   111
as sea see eve Lee/eel* eels*/else* seal/ sale*
save slave elves* leave easel* leaves

66. letters *s rs* (plural) *est eet west pest beets sheet* 112
see set let rest test tree reel else trees/
reset steel/sleet street settle* letter tester* lètters

67. longest *g n t s* (plural) *ot one trot bone*   113
phone cots
go no so to ton/not got set nest note/tone
lone long notes/tones longest

68. macaroni *r c m am an ain* (compound word)   114
plan ram vain plain
an am ram ran man can car/arc cram main
rain corn acorn manic* maniac* airman* macaroni

69. **machines** *h m ch s* (plural) *am an in ain spin* 115
tram plan plain
is in an am ham him his aim men man
main name same came chin/inch China*/chain
chime* chimes* inches machines

70. **Madeline** *m n l ed* (ending)* *an aid* ail* end* 116
maid-made paid trail* lend spend*
in an am mad man men end and aim* aid*
ail* mail* main* maid* made mend mean/name
nail* land lean* lead* line medal lined aimed*
named* ailed mailed* nailed* leaned limeade*
Madeline

71. **magnetic** *m ing* (ending) *an at eat ame clan* 117
spat treat lame
an am at mat man ant act* eat meat
mean*/mane* mine* mint* name game giant
magnet acting eating magnetic

72. **mammals** *m s s* (plural) *al am* (Names) *jam* 118
scram pal Val
as am Al Sam Sal mama slam alas mamas
mammal mammals

73. **manners** *m n s* (plural) *an ear ame fear spear* 119
games plans
an am me men man ran are/ear near/earn
mean/name same names smear manner
manners

74. **matter** *m t er* (ending) *am at eat flat seat* 120
pleat beater
am at mat/tam tar/rat eat/tea term meat/mate
rate/tear tame tamer treat matter

75. **measure** *s ear s* (plural) *see-sea seam-seem* 121
near spear flea glee
us me see sea ear/are arm arms seam* seem*
ears smear erase* reuse* resume* measure

76. **nature** *n r at an eat ear brat scat* 122
feat clear
at an ran rat rut nut net eat ear near neat
tear rent runt rate nature

77. **nuclear** *c l cl un* (prefix) *ean ear bean fear*   123
smear unclean
an can car are/ear near real care cane lean
clean clear unreal unclear/nuclear

78. **orange** *r an ag ear* age* plan wag*   124
smear stage**
or on an ran rag nag ear*/are* age* rage*
rang near* gear* range/anger organ*/groan* orange

79. **ornament** *m n am ear eat slam clear*   125
smear feat
or on am ram/arm are/ear eat neat meat
near mean* meant* manner remnant* ornament

80. **overcast** *c r v at ate est* (compound word) *scat*   126
late skate west
at rat rot ate rate race cast rest vest east
over cover voter votes roast overcast

81. **painter** *p at art et flat vet scat rent*   127
an at rat/art pat pet net/ten tan pan pant part
pair pain paint parent painter

82. **parties/pirates** *p r s* (plural) *at ip est aise**   128
ripe-riper-ripest hat slip test vest*
as at Pat rat rap rip tip/pit pet pets/pest rest
part rate* ripe* rise* arise*/raise* paste* parts
riper* pirate praise* ripest* pirates/parties

83. **pasta** *s sp t s* (plural) *ap at flat splat*   129
naps snap
as at sat pat/tap sap/spa spat/past/pats/taps
pasta

84. **patterns** *p s s* (plural) *at et flat vet*   130
nets parents
as an at pat sat set pet pen tens pens
pats/past pant* pants parts paste* patter*
parent patterns

85. **penguins** *p s s* (plural) *in ine* shin vine*   131
twin whine
in pin pen peg pig pigs pins pens pine*
unpin using* spine* genius* penguin penguins

86. **Pilgrims** *p r g s s* (plural) *ig ip trip skip*   132
wigs twig
is sip lip rip rig pig pigs slip/lips grip girl
girls prism* Pilgrims

87. **piñata** *p t at in it ant flat kin spit plant*   133
at it in pin pit/tip tap/pat pan ant pant pint
pain paint piñata

88. **planting** *p t pl an ail* ain* scan trail**   134
stain trailing*
an it pan/nap ant/tan plan pail* nail* tail*
pain* gain* giant* plant paint* plain* planting

89. **playing** *p l pl ing* (ending) *an ay in ain scan*   135
twin tray stain
in an pan pin pig pay lay play plan pain gain
plain paying laying playing

90. **practice** *p r pr at it art act ice spit chart*   136
fact twice
at it pit pat rat/art car act ice rice ripe*
part pact react* price pirate* carpet practice

91. **Prancer** *c p r an ap ape ace* scan nap*   137
scrape place
an pan can ran rap cap ape cape race*
pace* pacer* racer* pecan prance Prancer

92. **presents** *p pr r s ent est vent spent*   138
west crest
pen pet set see seen sent rent rest pest/step*
steps*/pests press* rents preset* resent*
present presents

93. **pretzels** *p r pr sl et est eel eep net vest*   139
steel creep
see set pet pets/pest rest reel peel peels/sleep
sleet* steep* reset* preset*/pester pretzels

94. **prince** *p r pr in ice spin twin slice twice*   140
in pin pen pie ice rip rice ripe* pier* pine*
nice nicer ripen* price prince

95. **puddles** *p s s* (plural) *ue us ed bus clue*
fled beds
up us use/Sue due led sled sped dues*/used*
plus pulse* puddle puddles

141

96. **pulleys** *p s sp s* (plural) *ell us y fell bells*
bus sky
up us use/sue yes spy sly sell yell yelp pull
plus pulse spell yells pulley pulleys

142

97. **puppies** *p s s* (plural) *up sips cup cups*
is us up pup pep sip Sue/use pie pies pipe
pups pipes puppies

143

98. **quilts** *l qu s* (plural) *it fit spit split hits*
is it lit sit/its slit/list suit quit quits quilt quilts

144

99. **raccoon** *r c an on orn Don born*
morn clan
on an can ran Ron car/arc oar corn acorn
cocoa croon raccoon

145

100. **railroad** *r l id ail* (compound word) *slid skid*
pail snail
as or our* rod rid lid aid* ail rail raid
road roar lord* load radar* radio* radial*
railroad

146

101. **rainbow** *b br w an orn* ain*
(compound word) *plan torn* scorn* train*
on an ran row bow air war warn worn*
born* barn rain brain brown robin* rainbow

147

102. **rainfall** *f r fr an air ail* (compound word)
Fran chair snail trail
in an ran fan far fir air fair fail rail rain*
fall* frail frill flair final* rainfall

148

103. **Ramona** *m r am an van plan ham slam*
or on an am ram/arm man ran roam moan
morn*/norm* aroma* manor Ramona

149

104. **recycle** *r c y* (two sounds) *s* (plural) *eel try*
sly heel wheel
cry rye eye eel reel rely eery* leery* cycle
celery* cycler recycle

150

105. **reptiles** *r s t s* (plural) *it ip est skit split*
vest snip
is it sit pit/tip rip pet pets/pest rest ripe
rips reel* reels* repel* reset preset* ripest
replies* reptiles 151

106. **rewards/drawers** *d r dr w ed aw ear jaw*
slaw fled hear
Ed red ear was/saw raw draw dear/read rear
draws reward/drawer drawers/rewards 152

107. **Rudolph** *h l r op old our oud our-hour**
*flop mold scold scour**
do up hop rod old our* hour* lord* hold
drop loud proud* uphold/holdup Rudolph 153

108. **science** *s sc s* (plural) *in ice seen-scene pin*
skin dice slice
is in see ice ices nice seen scene since*
niece* nieces scenic* science 154

109. **seasons** *s n s* (plural) *o nos-nose go yo*
pro pros
as an on/no so son one sea seas sons
ones/nose noses season seasons 155

110. **seedling** *s l sl ing* (ending) *id end ing**
*skid bend spend swing**
in is see end/den lid leg legs send slid
sing*/sign* slide sling* seeing seeding seedling 156

111. **shapes/phases** *h s ape ash* e ea we drape*
lash crash**
as he she sea pea/ape has*/ash* sash* seas
peas shape ashes* phase phases/shapes 157

112. **sleigh** *g l h s* (plural) *e is me we sleighs*
is hi he she his lie gel/leg legs/gels sigh
lies sleigh 158

113. **slept/pelts** *p s s* (plural) *et met vet sets steps*
let set pet pets/step/pest pelt pelts/slept 159

114. **smelling** *m l sl sm ing* (ending) *ile ime ine**
ingle dime crime whine* shingle**
me men see leg legs line lime/mile mine*
slim slime/smile smell sling* single* mingle*
selling smelling 160

115. snowball *b bl s sn s* (plural) *aw ow jaw*   161
claw show crows
as was/saw law low bow bowl/blow slow snow
ball balls bowls/blows blown sallow* snowball

116. snowman *s sn sw am an ow own* jam*   162
*slow scan known**
so no am an man Sam saw sow won/now/own*
sown*/snow swan swam woman snowman

117. snowy *n s sn s* (plural) *y on own ton*   163
sons grown blown
no now/own/won son/nos nosy snow/sown/owns
snowy

118. sorting/storing *s st r str ing* (ending) *ot ong*   164
ing plot wrong swing swinging
so to in or rot got not/ton tong song sing
ring sting string strong storing/sorting

119. spring *p gr s* (plural) *in ip ing twin hips*   165
slip fling
in pin pig sip rip rips grip grin/ring sing
spin rings spring

120. sprinkle *s sk sp ip in ink chin clip trip wink*   166
is in pin ink ski sir* sip snip/spin skin/sink
slip skip spike spine* skier* silken* sinker*
sprinkle

121. sprout *p t r op ot out ort drop hot*   167
*shout fort**
to top/pot rot rut out post port* pout rout
stop/spot/tops sport* spout spurt* sprout

122. stories *s t st s* (plural) *it ir ore fit fir*   168
more score
is it sit sir set toe tore sore sort* stir
store stores/sorest* sister* stories

123. stormy *t m st oy y* (two pronunciations)   169
(Names) *boy joy sky fly*
or my try toy Roy Tom rot sort toys
Troy most storm story stormy

124. subtract *s t ab at ar ub grab scat jar scrub*   170
us as at sat bat/tab tub sub stub stab star
scar start strut/trust subtract

125. summer   *m   s   use   um   gum   hum   plum   fuse**   171
me   us   use/sue   sum   rum   sure/user   muse*
serum*   summer

126. sunlight   *s   sl   st   s* (plural)   *ing   ight   ung**   172
(compound word)   *bring   might   flight   stings*
is   it   sit   sun   sung*   sing   sling   sting   stung*
sight   night   light   slight   nights   lights   sunlight

127. sunshine   *h   s   sh   s* (plural*)   in   ine   skin   spin*   173
spine   vines
in   us   sun   she   his   hen   hens   nine   shin*
shine   sinus   shines   wisher*   sunshine

128. table   *b   l   t   ab   at   ate   eat   able   cab   plate*   174
wheat   able
at   bat/tab   lab   let   bet   tea/eat/ate   late/
tale/teal   belt   beat   able   table

129. tacos   *c   s* (plural)   *at   oat   flat   splat*   175
float   goats
as   at   sat   cat/act   oat   cot   coat   cost
cast/cats/scat   oats   coats/coast/tacos

130. teaser   *s   t   tr   ee   eat   sea-see   what   pleat*   176
knee   treat
as   at   sat   set   see   sea   eat   seat/east   ears
star   tear*   tree   tears*   tease*   tears   reset*
eater   eaters/teaser*

131. terrible   *b   t   et   ie   net   vet   die   pie*   177
it   bit   bet   let   lie   tie   tire   tile   bite   belt   tribe/
biter   retire   terrible

132. trucks/struck   *c   r   t   s* (plural)   *ut   uck   ust   nut*   178
strut   luck   trust
us   rut   cut   cuts   ruts/rust   suck   tuck   truck
tucks   stuck   crust   struck/trucks

133. turkeys   *r   y   tr   s* (plural)   *y   ue   blue   glue*   179
dry   fly
us   use/Sue   yes   yet   try   sky   try   rut
ruts/rust   rest   true   keys   rusty   turkey   turkeys

134. umbrella *b bl m am ame all ear slam stall*   180
smear tame
am ram/arm rub bar ear all ball bell
bull blue dear mule* lame bluer blame
mural* rumble* ramble* lumber
marble* umbrella

135. valentine *v l an ate ine plan skate*   181
shine spine
it at an van tan/ant let ate late lane line
vine even* event* eaten* leave valentine

136. watering *w wr er**(ending) *ing* (ending) *an*   182
van plan wanting waiting
at an ant/tan ate*/eat ear want went wait*
wear tear water write twine* anger* waiter*
writer wearing tearing watering

137. weather *h th w wh er* (ending) *at ear eat*   183
here-hear wear-where that near meat beat
at rat ear eat heat hear here wear tear tree
three/there where wheat eater* heater* weather

138. whales *s l s* (plural) *aw ale claw draw*   184
scale scales
as has/ash was/saw law sea seal*/sale
slaw/laws wash heal heals/leash whale whales

139. whisper *h s w wh ip ipe slip clip pipe ripe*   185
is his hip rip sip sir ship whip wish wipe
wise wiser wiper swipe wipers wisher whisper

140. zucchini *ch z in inch win spin pinch finch*   186
hi in inch/chin chic zinc cinch zucchini

L E T T E R S

a c l p s

M A K E

Give children clues about how many letters to use. For example, "Now we're going to make some two-letter words. Hold up two fingers!" Then tell how many letters to add or change: "Add one letter to the word *Al*, a name, and make the three-letter word *pal*, as in 'You are my *pal*'." Remind children that when they have words like *pal/lap*, they only have to change the letters around to make the word *pal* into the new word *lap*. For the words *slap* and *clap*, have children stretch out each word to hear all the sounds. When you get to the secret (last) word, ask children if they can figure out the word they can make with all the letters. Say, "Use all your letters to make the secret word."

as	pal/	slap	claps
Al	lap	clap	
	cap		
	sap		

S O R T

s   c   Al   ap

T R A N S F E R

"What if you were **reading** and came to these words?" (Show *map* and *gap* printed on index cards but do not say the words.) "Which words that we made have the same spelling pattern and would help you read these words?" Have children put the index cards under the rhyming words and let the children use the words to figure out these two new words.

"What if you were **writing** and wanted to write *nap*. Which words rhyme with *nap*?" Let children help you spell *nap* using the *ap* pattern. Do the same for the word *hit*.

L E T T E R S

a d n s t

M A K E

Give children clues about how many letters to use. For example, "Now we're going to make some two-letter words. Hold up two fingers!" Then tell how many letters to change: "Just add one letter at the end of *an* and you can change the word *an* into *ant*—'See that tiny *ant*'." Remind children, "When you have words like *ant/tan*, you only have to change the letters around to make the word *ant* into the new word *tan*." When you ask students to make a word that is a proper name, remember to check and see if they use the capital letter. For the secret (last) word say, "Can you use all your letters to make the secret word for today?"

at	ant	sand	stand
as	tan		
an	Dan		
	and		

S O R T

s   an   and

T R A N S F E R

"What if you were **reading** and came to these words?" (Show *pan* and *hand* written on index cards but do not say the words.) "Which words that we made have the same spelling pattern and would help you read these words?" Have children put the index cards under the rhyming words and let the children use the words to figure out these two new words.

"What if you were **writing** and wanted to write the word *man*. Which words rhyme with *man*?" Let children help you spell *man* using the *an* pattern. Do the same for the word *band*.

LETTERS

e d n s t

MAKE

Give children clues about how many letters to use. For example, "Now we're going to make some three-letter words. Hold up three fingers!" Then tell children, "You only have to change the letters around to make the word *end* into the new three-letter word *den*." Also remind children which letters to change: "Change the first letter and you can change the word *den* into *ten*." Let children know when they need to stretch the word out to listen where to put the new letter: "Add a letter to *net* to make the four-letter word *nest*." Say the word *nest*, stretching it out. "Can you hear where you will put the new letter to make *nest*?" Finally say, "Use all your letters and see if you can make the secret word for today."

Ed	end/	nest	dents
	den	sent	
	ten	dent	
	set		
	net		

SORT

d   n   en   et   ent

TRANSFER

"What if you were **reading** and came to these words?" (Show *bet* and *bent* written on index cards but do not say the words.) "Which words that we made have the same spelling pattern and would help you read these words?" Have children put the index cards under the rhyming words and use the words to figure out these two new words.

"What if you were **writing** and wanted to write *pen*; which words rhyme with *pen*?" Let children help you spell *pen* using the *en* pattern. Do the same for the word *tent*.

LESSON 4

LETTERS

e d n p s

MAKE

Give children clues about how many letters to use: "Now we're going to make some three-letter words. Hold up three fingers!" Tell children, "Change just the first letter and you can change the word *den* into *pen*." When making the names *Ed* and *Ned*, check that students use capital letters for the *E* and the *N*. Remind students that sometimes they do not have to take any letters out, they can just change the letters around. "Change the letters around and you can change *end* to *Ned—Ned* is a new boy in our class." For the secret (last) word say, "See if you can use all your letters and make the secret word for today."

Ed	end	pens	spend
	Ned	dens	
	den	send	
	pen		

SORT

d　s　p　ed　en　end

TRANSFER

"What if you were **reading** and came to these words?" (Show *fed* and *bend* written on index cards but do not say the words.) "Which words that we made have the same spelling pattern and would help you read these words?" Have children put the index cards under the rhyming words and use the words to figure out these two new words.

"What if you were **writing** and wanted to write *bed*? Which words rhyme with *bed*?" Let children help you spell *bed* using the *ed* pattern. Do the same for the word *men*.

LETTERS

i h n s t

MAKE

Give children clues about how many letters to use: "Now we're going to make some three-letter words. Hold up three fingers!" Then tell children how many letters to change: "Change the first and last letters and you can change the word *tin* into *sit*," or "Change just the first letter and you can change *sit* into *hit*." Have children say the words and listen to the sounds they hear in the words. "Say the four-letter word *hint* (stretch it out); can you hear all four letters in that word?" For the last word you will make, say, "Add one letter to *hint* for our secret word for today."

is   tin   hits   hints
it   sit   hint
in   hit

SORT

s   h   it   in

TRANSFER

"What if you were **reading** and came to these words?" (Show *fin* and *bit* written on index cards but do not say the words.) "Which words that we made have the same spelling pattern and would help you read these words?" Have children put the index cards under the rhyming words and use the words to figure out these two new words.

"What if you were **writing** and wanted to write *pin*; which words rhyme with *pin*?" Let children help you spell *pin* using the *in* pattern. Do the same for the word *hit*.

LESSON 6

LETTERS

i l p s t

MAKE

Give children clues about how many letters to use: "Now we're going to make some two-letter words. Hold up two fingers!" Then tell how many letters to change: "Change just the last letter and you can change the word *is* into *it*." Remind children, "When you have a word like *slip* or *spit*, stretch out the word and listen to all the letter sounds you hear in this four-letter word." When making the last word say, "Use all your letters to make the secret word for today."

is	sit	slip	split
it	pit	spit	
	tip		
	sip		
	lip		

SORT

s   it   ip

TRANSFER

"What if you were **reading** and came to these words?" (Show *rip* and *bit* written on index cards but do not say the words.) "Which words that we made have the same spelling pattern and would help you read these words?" Have children put the index cards under the rhyming words. Encourage children to use the words to figure out these two new words.

"What if you were **writing** and wanted to write *dip*; which words rhyme with *dip*?" Let children help you spell *dip* using the *ip* pattern. Do the same for the word *hit*.

LETTERS

o f g r s

MAKE

Give children clues about how many letters to use: "Now we're going to make some two-letter words. Hold up two fingers!" Then tell how many letters to change: "Change just the first letter, and you can change the word *no* into *so*;" and "Change just the last letter, and you can change the word *for* into *fog*—'It is hard to see in the morning *fog*'." Have children speak the word *frog*, stretching out the four letters so that they can hear all the sounds in the word, then make the word. For the last word say, "Use all your letters and make the secret word for today, which has five letters."

no	for	frog	frogs
so	fog		
go			
or			

SORT

f   o   or   og

TRANSFER

"What if you were **reading** and came to these words?" (Show *hog* and *log* written on index cards but do not say the words.) "Which words that we made have the same spelling pattern and would help you read these words?" Have children put the index cards under the rhyming words and use the words to figure out these two new words.

"What if you were **writing** and wanted to write *bog*; which words rhyme with *bog*?" Let children help you spell *bog* using the *og* pattern.

L·E·T·T·E·R·S

<h2 style="text-align:center">o p r s t</h2>

M·A·K·E

Give children clues about how many letters to use: "Now we're going to make some three-letter words. Hold up three fingers!" Then tell how many letters to change: "Change just the first letter, and you can change the word *rot* into *pot*." Remind children, "When you have words like *pots*, *post*, *stop*, and *spot*, you only have to change the letters around to make the word *pots* into the word *post*, then into *stop* and *spot*." For an unusual word like *pro*, give children a sentence to help them understand the meaning: "Michael Jordan plays *pro* basketball."

so	pro	pots/	sport
	rot	post/	
	pot	stop/	
		spot	

S·O·R·T

<h3 style="text-align:center">s   p   o   ot</h3>

T·R·A·N·S·F·E·R

"What if you were **reading** and came to these words?" (Show *go* and *hot* written on index cards but do not say the words.) "Which words that we made have the same spelling pattern and would help you read these words?" Have children put the index cards under the rhyming words and use the words to figure out these two new words.

"What if you were **writing** and wanted to write *got*; which words rhyme with *got*?" Let children help you spell *got* using the *ot* pattern. Do the same for the word *no*.

L E T T E R S

u g n s t

M A K E

Give children clues about how many letters to use: "Now we're going to make some three-letter words. Hold up three fingers!" Tell how many letters to change: "Change just the last letter and you can change the word *gun* into the word *gut*—a man's *gut* is his stomach." "Change just the first letter of *gut* and you have a new word, *nut*." Check to see if children use the capital *G* for the first letter of the name *Gus*. Remember to have the children stretch out the words *snug* and *stun* to hear all the letter sounds. For the final word you make, say, "Now use all your letters to make the secret word for today."

us	Gus	snug	stung
	gun	stun	
	gut		
	nut		
	tug		

S O R T

s   g   us   un   ug   ut

T R A N S F E R

"What if you were **reading** and came to these words?" (Show *bus* and *run* written on index cards but do not say the words.) "Which words that we made have the same spelling pattern and would help you read these words?" Have the children put the index cards under the rhyming words and use the words to figure out these two new words.

"What if you were **writing** and wanted to write *rug*; which words rhyme with *rug*?" Let children help you spell *rug* using the *ug* pattern. Do the same for the word *but*.

L E T T E R S

u h n s t

M A K E

Give children clues about how many letters to use: "Now we're going to make some three-letter words. Hold up three fingers!" Tell children how many letters to change: "Change just the first letter, and you can change the word *nut* into *hut*." For words like *nuts* and *stun*, which can be made from the same letters, tell children, "Don't take any letters out. Just change the letters around, and you can change *nuts* into *stun*." Give children meanings they might understand as you ask them to make the words. For example, "The light will *stun* the animal and stop him." For the last word you will make, always let students try to figure it out: "Now use all your letters and make the secret word for today."

us	sun	huts	hunts
	nut	nuts/	
	hut	stun	
		hunt	

S O R T

s   h   un   ut

T R A N S F E R

"What if you were **reading** and came to these words?" (Show *cut* and *bun* written on index cards but do not say the words.) "Which words that we made have the same spelling pattern and would help you read these words?" Have children put the index cards under the rhyming words and use the words to figure out these two new words.

"What if you were **writing** and wanted to write *run*; which words rhyme with *run*?" Let children help you spell *run* using the *un* pattern. Do the same for the word *rut*.

LETTERS

a o c n r s

A good lesson for the fall season!

MAKE

on	ran	cars	acorn	acorns
or	can	cans/	corns/	
as	car	scan	scorn	
an		corn		

SORT

c   sc   s (plural)   an   orn

TRANSFER

van   horn   scan   pans

LESSON 2

LETTERS

a i d d g n

You can do this lesson any day you are adding
during a math lesson.

MAKE

in	add	ding	adding
an	aid	gain	
ad	and		
	dad		
	did		
	dig		
	nag		

SORT

d   ad   ad-add

TRANSFER

pad   sad   mad   glad

LETTERS

a a e i l n p r

MAKE

an	pin	pair*	plane/	airplane
in	pen	pail*	panel	
	pan	pain	plain*	
	ran	rain	ripen*	
	rap	rail*	alien*	
	rip	ripe		
	air*	plan		

SORT

p   pl   r   an   in   ain   ail*

TRANSFER

spin   fail*   scan   stain

LESSON 4

LETTERS

a a e b h l p t

This is a good lesson after reading an alphabet book
or learning alphabetical order!

MAKE

at	pat	late	plate/	alphabet
	hat	hate/	petal*	
	bat	heat*	table*	
	bet	heal*		
	let	help*		
	pet			
	ate			

SORT

b   h   at   et   ate

TRANSFER

slat   vet   brat   get

50

LETTERS

a o h n n t y

This is a good lesson to follow the story
Big Anthony by Tomie DePaola.

MAKE

an	hat	oath*	Anthony
on	hot	than	
at	not		
	tan/		
	ant		
	any		
	toy*		
	oat*		

SORT

h t an at ot

TRANSFER

plan lot tan flat

LESSON 6

LETTERS

a i r s t t

MAKE

at	sit	tart	artist	artists
as	sir	star	stairs	
is	sat	stir		
it	rat/			
	art/			
	tar			

SORT

s   st   t   s (plural)   at   art   ir

TRANSFER

scat   fir   part   start

LETTERS

a o u h r t

A good lesson to do when reading books by any author.

MAKE

at	our	hurt	author
or	out	hour	
	art/	tour/	
	tar	rout	
	hat	auto	
	hot		
	hut		

SORT

h   t   at   our   out

our-hour

TRANSFER

brat   sour   pout   snout

LESSON 8

a u u m n t

This is a seasonal word to be used when learning about the seasons or during autumn or for any story set in the fall; for example, *Frederick* by Leo Leoni.

MAKE

an	mat/	tuna/	autumn
am	tam	aunt	
at	man		
	ant/		
	tan		
	nut		

SORT

m   t   am   an   at

TRANSFER

slam   vat   ram   plan

54

LETTERS

a o o b h m r t

MAKE

at	bat	root	booth	bathroom
	mat	room	broom	
	rat	boot	robot	
	rot	bath		
		both		

SORT

b   r   at   oot   oom

TRANSFER

flat   zoom   gloom   loot

LESSON 10

LETTERS

a e e b r s v

MAKE

be	bee	bear/	brave	beaver	beavers
	bar	bare	erase*		
	are/	save	verse*/		
	ear	vase*	serve*		
		rave*			

SORT

b   v   ave   ase*   bear/bare

TRANSFER

she   gave   slave   case*

56

LETTERS

e o o b d m r

This is a good word to use while reading
Ira Sleeps Over by Bernard Waber.

MAKE

do	bed	rode	bored	bedroom
	red	robe	broom	
	rod	room	rodeo	
	rob	doom		
		door		
		more		
		bore		

SORT

b   d   r   ed   oom   ore

TRANSFER

bled   sled   zoom   store

LESSON 12

LETTERS

a i b d h r t y

MAKE

at	bit	bird	braid	birthday
it	bid	bath	birth	
	hid	hard	dairy*/	
	day	yard	diary*	
	ray	raid		

SORT

b h r br id ay aid

TRANSFER

skit stay card paid

LETTERS

e i u b n n s

This is a good word to make during the spring holidays.

MAKE

in   bus   buns   bunnies
us   bin   bins
       sun   nine
       sub   snub

SORT

b   s   in   us   ub

TRANSFER

win   spin   cub   Gus

LESSON 14

oubnstt

MAKE

us	bus	bout	stunt	button	buttons
but	bust	stout			
nut	nuts/	snout			
out	stun	bonus			

SORT

b   us   ut   out

TRANSFER

cut   strut   pout   shout

LETTERS

a i c g m n p

MAKE

am	can	camp	magic	pacing	camping
an	cap	main	manic		
	nap/	pain	panic		
	pan	gain			
	man				
	map				

SORT

c   m   ing (ending)   an   ap   ain

TRANSFER

plan   trap   snap   gaining

LESSON 16

LETTERS

a e c l s t

MAKE

at	cat	seat*	tales/	castle
	sat	scat/	stale/	
	set	cats/	steal*	
	let	cast	scale	
	eat*	sale		
		tale		

SORT

c   s   sc   s (plural)   at   et   eat*   ale

TRANSFER

jet   vet   beat*   scales

LETTERS

e e i c g h n r

MAKE

in	hen	rice	cheer	enrich	cheering
he	her	nice	hinge		
	ice	ring	green		
		rich	nicer		
		inch			
		here			

SORT

h   r   ch   ice

TRANSFER

dice   twice   spice

LETTERS

e i c c h k n

This word can be used after reading stories about chickens, including old favorites like *Chicken Little* by Beverly Burgess.

MAKE

in	hen	hick	chick	chicken
hi	Ken	nick	check	
he	kin	neck		

SORT

h   k   n   en   in   eck   ick

TRANSFER

when   slick   peck   then

LETTERS

i o c d f f l r

This is a wonderful word to make when reading stories written by Norman Bridwell about Clifford the big red dog.

MAKE

or	off	foil	cliff	Clifford
if	for	coil		
	fir	cord		
	old	cold		
	oil	fold		
		Ford		

SORT

c   f   old   oil   ord   (Names)

TRANSFER

sold   scold   spoil   lord

LESSON 20

o c l n s w

MAKE

on	cow	sown/	clown	clowns
	owl/	snow	scowl	
	low	slow/		
	now/	owls		
	own	cows		

SORT

c   cl   **ow** (two pronunciations)

own (two pronunciations)

TRANSFER

blow   how   show   shown

LETTERS

e o c n s t t

MAKE

no	tot	cone	notes	contest
to	cot	cost	cones	
	not	cent	cents	
	one	sent		
		ones		
		nest		
		test		
		note		

SORT

c (two sounds)   n   s (plural)   ent   est   ot

Help the children see that c can make two sounds.

TRANSFER

spot   vest   spent   crest

LESSON 22

o o u c d r r y

This is a good word to choose when you read stories
about Corduroy, written by Don Freeman.

MAKE

do	rod	door/	Corduroy
or	cod	odor	
	coy	cord	
	Roy		
	dry		
	cry		

SORT

c   r   y   od   oy

TRANSFER

sod   clod   fly   toy

68

LETTERS

i o u c g n n t

This is a wonderful word to make when reading counting books or
learning to count during your math time!

MAKE

in	got	into	count	tuning	counting
to	cot	unit	tonic*	toning*	
	cut	coin*	tunic*	outing	
	out		union*		

SORT

c   t   ing (ending)   ot

If you think your students are ready, teach them about doubling the
consonant before adding -ing to words such as cut.

TRANSFER

rot   slot   going   cutting*

LESSON 24

LETTERS

o c d r s w

MAKE

do	sod	cows	words/	crowds
so	cod	rows	sword	
	rod	crow	crowd	
	row	cord	crows	
	cow	word	cords	

SORT

c   cr   r   w   s (plural)   **od**   **ow** (two sounds)

TRANSFER

pod   blow   glow   how

LETTERS

a i u c n r t

MAKE

in	can	cart	train	curtain
an	tan	runt/		
	ran	turn		
	run	tuna		
	rut	rain		
	cut			
	car			

SORT

c   r   t   un   ut   ain (two pronunciations)

TRANSFER

shut   Stan   main   plain

LESSON 26

LETTERS

a e c d n r

Dancer begins with a capital *D* because it's the name of one of Santa's reindeer!

MAKE

an	red	dear	cared/	Dancer
Ed	ran	near	raced	
	can	cane*	dance*	
	car	card		
	end/	care		
	den			
	ear			

SORT

r   c   d   ed (ending)   an   ear

TRANSFER

van   plan   spear   speared

LETTERS

a e d h r s

(two secret words)

Dasher begins with a capital *D* because it's the name
of one of Santa's reindeer!

MAKE

as	has	hear	reads	shared/
had	herd	hears		Dasher
sad	rash	heard		
her	dash	share		
ear	read			

SORT

h r sh ad ash ear

herd-heard

TRANSFER

glad cash trash clear

LESSON 28

LETTERS

a e e o c d r t

MAKE

or	cat	dear	crate	create	created	decorate
at	ate/	deer	eater			
	eat	date				
	ear	rate				
		card				
		care				

SORT

c   d   ear   ate

deer-dear

TRANSFER

fear   smear   gate   plate

L E T T E R S

e e e i c d t t v

This is a great word to use when reading mysteries.

M A K E

it	tie	rice	detect	deceive*	detective
	die	dice	devise*		
	ice	diet*/			
		tide*/			
		tied*/			
		edit*			

S O R T

d   t   de*   ie   ice
tied/tide

T R A N S F E R

lie   nice   twice   defer*

LESSON 30

LETTERS

a i o u d n r s

MAKE

is	our*	soar*	irons*	around	dinosaur
in	son	sour*	radio*		
on	sun	rain	round		
or*	run	ruin*	sound		
	sir	iron*			
	air*				
	oar*				

SORT

s   r   un   oar*   our*   ound

TRANSFER

gun   stun   boar   found

76

LETTERS

e i o c d r s v

MAKE

is	ice	side/	drive/	covers*	discover
	sir	dies	diver	drives/	
		disc	dives	divers	
		dice	drove		
		dive	disco*		
			cover*		

SORT

s   d   dr   s (plural)   ice   ive

TRANSFER

nice   spice   live   hives

LESSON 32

LETTERS

a o d g n r s

MAKE

an	and	sang	grand	dragon	dragons
	ran	drag	drags		
	rag	rang			
	sag	sang			
	nag	sand			

SORT

s   r   dr   ag   ang   and

TRANSFER

bag   snag   bang   brand

LETTERS

i u c d g k l n

This is a good word to use after reading *Make Way for the Ducklings* by Robert McCloskey or studying about animals in a science theme.

MAKE

in	kin/	duck	cling	ducking	duckling
ink	luck	clink			
kid	lick				
lid	king				
dig					
dug					

SORT

d   l   cl   in   id   ing   ink   uck

TRANSFER

stuck   sting   spin   slid

LESSON 34

LETTERS

a e h r t

MAKE

he	hat	hate/	Earth
at	rat/	heat	
	art	rate	
	eat/		
	ate		

SORT

h r ate eat

TRANSFER

gate plate seat treat

LETTERS

e e i c c l r t

MAKE

it	lit	rice	liter*	electric
	let	lice	elect	
	tie	tile	erect*	
	lie	tire*		
	ice	tree		
		tier*		

SORT

l   t   ie   it   ice

TRANSFER

die   knit   vice   twice

LESSON 36

LETTERS

a e e c p s

MAKE

as   see   cape/   space/   escape
        sea   pace   capes
        pea/   peas/
        ape   apes
        ace
        cap

SORT

s   p   ea   ape   ace
see-sea

TRANSFER

flea   tape   lace   trace

LETTERS

a i f l m y

MAKE

am	fly	mail	filmy	family
if	Fay	fail		
my	may/	film		
	yam			
	aim			
	ail			

SORT

f   m   y   ail   ay

TRANSFER

spy   try   trail   stay

LESSON 38

LETTERS

e e e d f r s

This is a good word to use during a theme on birds or winter.

MAKE

Ed	red	seed	frees	feeder	feeders
	fed	deer	feeds	seeder	
	fee	feed			
	see	free			

SORT

f   s   s (plural)   er (ending)   ed   ee

TRANSFER

fled   flee   fees   sender

84

LETTERS

i i o c f n t

This is a good word to use any time you are reading fiction.

MAKE

if	fin	into	tonic	fiction
in	fit	info		
	not	font		
	cot	coin		
	not/			
	ton			
	tin			

SORT

c   f   t   in   ot

TRANSFER

shin   skin   spot   shot

LESSON 40

LETTERS

e i f g n r s

MAKE

is	fin	fine*	fines*	finger	fingers
in	fig	fire*	fires*/	singer	
	fir	grin/	fries*		
	sir	ring	rings/		
		sing/	grins		
		sign*			

SORT

f   s   gr   s (plural)   in   ir   ing

TRANSFER

twin   stir   sting   swings

LETTERS

a e f l m s

This is a word to use when studying fire safety.

MAKE

am	Sam	flea	flame	flames
	sea	self	fleas	
	elf	seal		
		seam		
		meal/		
		lame		
		same		
		fame		

SORT

c   s   fl   s (plural)   ea   eal   ame   elf

TRANSFER

tea   squeal   game   shelf

LETTERS

a e o c f r s t

This is a good word to use during a weather unit or theme.

MAKE

as	for	fear	crate	forces	forecast
at	far	feat	coast*	forest*	
of	fat	fast	force	faster	
	eat/	cast			
	ate	star			
	ear	rate			

SORT

f   ate   eat

TRANSFER

gate   slate   neat   treat

LETTERS

e i d f l n r y

This is a good word to use when reading a story about friends.

MAKE

if	fin	lend*	filed*	finder*	friendly
in	fir*	line	fined*	finely*	
	fly	fine	fired/	friend	
	fry	find	fried		
	dry	fire	field*		
	red	file*			
	end*				

SORT

f   fl   fr   ly*   ed (ending)   end*   in   ine

TRANSFER

kin   spin   dined   twine

LESSON 44

LETTERS

i u f r s t

This is a good word to use during a health theme.

MAKE

is	fit	furs	fruit	fruits
it	fir	firs	first	
	fur	fits/		
		fist/		
		sift		
		surf		
		turf		
		rust		

SORT

f   s   s (plural)   st   it   ir   urf

TRANSFER

kit   skit   post   Smurfs

LETTERS

a e d g n r s

This is a word to use during a planting theme or after a story about a garden.

MAKE

an	ran	gear	range*/	garden/	gardens
	rag	dear	anger*	danger*	
	age	aged	grand	ranges*	
	gas*	rage	grade		
	ear	rags			
		drag			
		rang*			

SORT

r   g   gr   s (plural)   er (ending)   ear   ag

TRANSFER

fear   flag   grades   ears

LETTERS

e e o g m r t y

We study geometry during Math—circles, squares, triangles, and more!

MAKE

me	got	Troy	greet	meteor*	geometry
go	get	tree	meter*		
	met	term			
	Tom	germ			
	Roy	meet			
	toy				
	try				

SORT

g   m   t   tr   oy   erm   eet

(Names)

TRANSFER

boy   perm   tweet   sweet

LETTERS

o g h s s t

This is a good word to use when reading stories about
Gus the Friendly Ghost or during October!

MAKE

so	got	hogs/	hosts/	ghosts
go	hot	gosh	shots	
	hog	shot/	ghost	
		host		

SORT

g   h   s (plural)   ot   ost

TRANSFER

trot   plot   post   posts

LESSON 48

a i g n s t

There are many good stories about giants—or perhaps you
are doing a fairy-tale theme!

MAKE

it	ant/	snag/	gains	giants
in	tan	sang	giant	
an	tin	sing/	stain/	
	sit	sign*	saint*/	
	sat	gain	satin*	
	sag			

SORT

t   g   s   s (plural)   in   it   ag   ain

TRANSFER

skit   wag   brain   stains

94

LETTERS

i o g g l n w

MAKE

in	win	glow	going	owning	glowing
	wig	long			
	log	lion			
	low/	wing			
	owl				
	own				

SORT

g   gl   l   w   ing (ending)   in

OW (two pronunciations)

TRANSFER

fin   shin   snow   snowing

LESSON 50

LETTERS

a e g p r s

MAKE

as	gas	rags	grape/	grapes
	gap	rage	pager	
	sap	page	pages	
	rap	gaps/	grasp*	
	rag	gasp*		

SORT

g   r   p   s (plural)   ap   age

TRANSFER

nap   snap   cage   stage

LETTERS

a i g g h n p r

MAKE

in	pin	rain	grain	paging	graphing
	pig	pain	graph*		
	gap	gain	aging		
	rap	grin			
	ran	grip*			

SORT

p   r   g   gr   ing (ending)   in   ap   ain

TRANSFER

trap   stain   slap   skin

LESSON 52

LETTERS

i o g g n r w

MAKE

on	win	grow	grown*	rowing	growing
in	won/	grin/	going		
	own	ring	wring*		
	row	wing			
		gown*			

SORT

w   r   g   gr   ing (ending)   in   ing   ow

ring-wring*

TRANSFER

twin   spin   slow   swing

LETTERS

a i u g r s t

MAKE

it   sat   grit   stair   stairs   guitars
at   rat/   stir   grits   guitar
      tar   star
      rag
      rug
      tug

SORT

r   t   st   s (plural)   at   ug   it   ar

TRANSFER

scat   jug   smug   skit

LESSON 54

LETTERS

a o d h l r

This is a good word for *Harold and the Purple Crayon* by Crockett Johnson or *Lizzie and Harold* stories, written by Elizabeth Winthrop.

MAKE

or	rod	lord	hoard	Harold
	old	load		
	oar	road		
	had	hold		
	lad	hard		

SORT

h   l   ad   old   oad

TRANSFER

mad   sold   scold   toad

LETTERS

a e h r t

MAKE

at	her	hate	heart
he	the	rate/	
	are	tear	
	ate/	hear	
	eat	heat	
	ear		
	rat		
	hat		

SORT

h   r   at   eat   ear   ate

Help your students understand the two pronunciations and meanings for *tear*.

TRANSFER

beat   plate   skate   smear

LETTERS

a i o d h l s y

You could do this lesson before or during any holiday.

MAKE

he	his	hold	daily	holiday	holidays
is	has/	sold	daisy		
	ash	load	shady		
	had	dash			
	hay	lash			
	lay	lady			
	old				

SORT

h   l   d   y   ay   old   ash

TRANSFER

stay   gold   rash   crash

LETTERS

e i o b h l r r

You could do this lesson after reading the book *Alexander and the Terrible, Horrible, No Good, Very Bad Day* by Judith Viorst or on any day that was going all wrong at school!

MAKE

he	rob	hero*	broil	broiler	horrible
or	rib	hole			
	oil	role*			
	hoe*	robe*			
	her	boil			

SORT

h   r   b   ole*   oil

TRANSFER

mole   stole   foil   spoil

LETTERS

e u d d h n r s

MAKE

he	red	herd	under	rushed	shudder*	hundreds
us	end/	send	udder*		hundred	
Ed	den	rush				
	hen					
	her					

SORT

h   r   ed   en   end

TRANSFER

fed   fled   when   spend

LETTERS

a i i d n n s

MAKE

as	inn	said	Indian	Indians
an	and/	sand		
in	Dan	inns		
	sad/			
	ads			
	aid			

SORT

s   s (plural)   an   and
in-inn

TRANSFER

van   plan   land   stand

LESSON 60

a e c j k s t

MAKE

as	cat/	task	jacks	jacket	jackets
at	act	cats/	stack	casket*	
	ask	cast	stake*/		
		cake	steak*		
		take	cakes		
		sake			
		sack			
		jack			

SORT

c   j   s   st*   s (plural)   ake   ack   ask

TRANSFER

flake   snack   smack   mask

106

LETTERS

a o u j l n r

You could do this lesson any day if your class is journal writing.

MAKE

or	Jan	oral*	lunar*	journal
on	ran	loan		
an	run			
	nor/			
	Ron			
	oar			
	our			

SORT

I   r   an   on   or   (Names)

TRANSFER

plan   for   Don   van

LETTERS

a a o o g k n r

This is a good lesson when reading
Katy No-Pocket by Emmy Payne or during an animal theme.

MAKE

an	Ron	rang	groan/	kangaroo
or	ran	rank	organ	
on	rag	okra		
	nag			

SORT

r   an   ag   on

TRANSFER

wag   upon   tag   plan

LETTERS

i o d g k m n

MAKE

on	kin/	kind	doing	kingdom
in	ink	king		
	dog	ding		
	dig	mind		
	kid	oink		

SORT

k   d   in   ind   ing

You may need to talk about the difference between the pattern *ing* in *king* and *ding* and the ending *ing* on *doing*.

TRANSFER

win   sing   swing   find

LESSON 64

LETTERS

i o c g k k n n

MAKE

in	non	kink	knock	knocking
go	inn	king		
no/	ink/	kick		
on	kin	Nick		
		coin*		
		oink*		

SORT

k   kn   in   ink   ick
in-inn

TRANSFER

twin   link   drink   flick

110

LETTERS

a e e l s v

MAKE

as	sea	eels*/	slave	leaves
	see	else*	elves*	
	eve	seal/	leave	
	Lee/	sale*	easel*	
	eel*	save		

SORT

s   l   s (plural)   ave   ee

see-sea

TRANSFER

pave   grave   tree   free

LESSON 66

LETTERS

e e l r s t t

MAKE

see	rest	trees/	street	letters
set	test	reset	settle*	
let	tree	steel/	letter	
	reel	sleet	tester*	
	else			

SORT

s   rs (plural)   est   eet

TRANSFER

west   pest   beets   sheet

LETTERS

e o g l n s t

This is a good word to use on a day when you are measuring in math.

MAKE

go	ton/	nest	notes/	longest
no	not	note/	tones	
so	got	tone		
to	set	lone		
		long		

SORT

g   n   t   s (plural)   ot   one

TRANSFER

trot   bone   phone   cots

LETTERS

a a i o c m n r

This word can be used during a health or foods unit.

MAKE

an	ram	cram	acorn	maniac*	macaroni
am	ran	main	manic*	airman*	
	man	rain			
	can	corn			
	car/				
	arc				

SORT

r   c   m   am   an   ain   (compound word)

TRANSFER

plan   ram   vain   plain

LETTERS

a e i c h m n s

This word can be used during a science unit on machines.

MAKE

is	ham	main	China*/	chimes*	machines
in	him	name	chain	inches	
an	his	same	chime*		
am	aim	came			
	men	chin/			
	man	inch			

SORT

h   m   ch   s (plural)   am   an   in   ain

TRANSFER

spin   tram   plan   plain

LETTERS

a e e i d l m n

MAKE

in	mad	mail*	medal	mailed*	limeade*	Madeline
an	man	main*	lined	nailed*		
am	men	maid*	aimed*	leaned		
	end	made	named*			
	and	mend	ailed			
	aim*	mean/				
	aid*	name				
	ail*	nail*				
		land				
		lean*				
		lead*				
		line				

SORT

m   n   l   ed (ending)*   an   aid*   ail*   end
maid-made

TRANSFER

paid*   trail*   lend   spend

LETTERS

a e i c g m n t

This word can be used during a science unit on magnets.

MAKE

an	mat	meat	giant	magnet	magnetic
am	man	mean*/		acting	
at	ant	mane*		eating	
	act*	mine*			
	eat	mint*			
		name			
		game			

SORT

m   ing (ending)   an   at   eat   ame

TRANSFER

clan   spat   treat   lame

LESSON 72

LETTERS

a a l m m s

This is a good lesson during a science theme on animals.

MAKE

as	Sam	mama	mamas	mammal	mammals
am	Sal	slam			
Al		alas			

SORT

m   s   s (plural)   al   am   (Names)

TRANSFER

jam   scram   pal   Val

LETTERS

a e m n n r s

MAKE

an	men	near/	names	manner	manners
am	man	earn	smear		
me	ran	mean/			
	are/	name			
	ear	same			

SORT

m　　n　　s (plural)　　an　　ear　　ame

TRANSFER

fear　　spear　　games　　plans

LESSON 74

LETTERS

a e m r t t

This word can be used after a science unit on matter.

MAKE

am	mat/	term	tamer	matter
at	tam	meat/	treat	
	tar/	mate		
	rat	rate/		
	eat/	tear		
	tea	tame		

SORT

m   t   er (ending)   am   at   eat

TRANSFER

flat   seat   pleat   beater

LETTERS

a e e u m r s

This word can be used during a science or math unit on measuring.

MAKE

us	see	arms	smear	resume*	measure
me	sea	seam*	erase*		
	ear/	seem*	reuse*		
	are	ears			
	arm				

SORT

s   ear   s (plural)
see-sea   seam-seem

TRANSFER

near   spear   flea   glee

LETTERS

a e u n r t

This word can be used during any nature unit or theme.

MAKE

at	ran	near	nature
an	rat	neat	
	rut	tear	
	nut	rent	
	net	runt	
	eat	rate	
	ear		

SORT

n   r   at   an   eat   ear

Help your students understand the two pronunciations and meanings for the word *tear.*

TRANSFER

brat   scat   feat   clear

LETTERS

a e u c l n r

MAKE

an	can	near	clean	unreal	unclear/
	car	real	clear		nuclear
	are/	care			
	ear	cane			
		lean			

SORT

c   l   cl   un (prefix)   ean   ear

TRANSFER

bean   fear   smear   unclean

LESSON 78

a e o g n r

MAKE

or	ran	rage*	range/	orange
on	rag	rang	anger	
an	nag	near*	organ*/	
	ear*/	gear*	groan*	
	are*			
	age*			

SORT

r   an   ag   ear*   age*

TRANSFER

plan   wag   smear*   stage*

124

LETTERS

a e o m n n r t

MAKE

or	ram/	neat	meant*	manner	ornament
on	arm	meat			
am	are/	near		remnant*	
	ear	mean*			
	eat				

SORT

m   n   am   ear   eat

TRANSFER

slam   clear   smear   feat

LETTERS

a e o c r s t v

This is a good word to use when learning about weather or the seasons!

MAKE

at	rat	rate	cover	overcast
	rot	race	voter	
ate	cast	votes		
	rest	roast		
	vest			
	east			
	over			

SORT

c   r   v   at   ate   est

(compound word)

TRANSFER

scat   late   skate   west

LETTERS

a e i n p r t

This is a good word to make after reading about an artist or painter.

MAKE

an	rat/	pant	paint	parent	painter
at	art	part			
	pat	pair			
	pet	pain			
	net/				
	ten				
	tan				
	pan				

SORT

p   at   art   et

TRANSFER

flat   vet   scat   rent

LETTERS

a e i p r s t

(two secret words)

MAKE

as	Pat	pets/	arise*/	pirate	pirates/
at	rat	pest	raise*	praise*	parties
	rap	rest	paste*	ripest*	
	rip	part	parts		
	tip/	rate*	riper*		
	pit	ripe*			
	pet	rise*			

SORT

p r s (plural) at ip est aise*

ripe-riper-ripest*

TRANSFER

hat slip test vest

LETTERS

a a p s t

Here is a word to make when reading
Strega Nona by Tomie DePaola or during a foods theme.

MAKE

as	sat	spat/	pasta
at	pat/	past/	
	tap	pats/	
	sap/	taps	
	spa		

SORT

s   sp   t   s (plural)   ap   at

TRANSFER

flat   splat   naps   snap

LETTERS

a e n p r s t t

MAKE

as	pat	tens	pants	patter*	patterns
an	sat	pens	parts	parent	
at	set	pats/	paste*		
	pet	past			
	pen	pant*			

SORT

p   s   s (plural)   at   et

TRANSFER

flat   vet   nets   parents

LETTERS

e i u g n n p s

This is a good lesson when reading
Tacky the Penguin by Helen Lester or for a science unit.

MAKE

in	pin	pigs	unpin	genius*	penguin	penguins
	pen	pins	using*			
	peg	pens	spine*			
	pig	pine*				

SORT

p   s   s (plural)   in   ine*

TRANSFER

shin   vine   twin   whine

LESSON 86

i i g l m p r s

MAKE

is	sip	pigs	girls	Pilgrims
	lip	slip/	prism*	
	rip	lips		
	rig	grip		
	pig	girl		

SORT

p   r   g   s   s (plural)   ig   ip

TRANSFER

trip   skip   wigs   twig

132

LETTERS

a a i n p t

Here is a holiday word!

MAKE

at	pin	pant	paint	piñata
it	pit/	pint		
in	tip	pain		
	tap/			
	pat			
	pan			
	ant			

SORT

p   t   at   in   it   ant

TRANSFER

flat   kin   spit   plant

LETTERS

a i g l n n p t

Use this word when learning about plants or planting a garden.

MAKE

an	pan/	plan	giant*	planting
it	nap	pail*	plant	
	ant/	nail*	paint*	
	tan	tail*	plain*	
		pain*		
		gain*		

SORT

p   t   pl   an   ail*   ain*

TRANSFER

scan   trail*   stain*   trailing

LETTERS

a i g l n p y

MAKE

in	pan	play	plain	paying	playing
an	pin	plan		laying	
	pig	pain			
	pay	gain			
	lay				

SORT

p   l   pl   ing (ending)   an   ay   in   ain

TRANSFER

scan   twin   tray   stain

LESSON 90

LETTERS

a e i c c p r t

MAKE

at	pit	rice	react*	pirate*	practice
it	pat	ripe*	price	carpet	
	rat/	part			
	art	pact			
	car				
	act				
	ice				

SORT

p   r   pr   at   it   art   act   ice

TRANSFER

spit   chart   fact   twice

136

LETTERS

a e c n p r r

Name a reindeer!

MAKE

an	pan	cape	pacer*	prance	Prancer
	can	race*	racer*		
	ran	pace*	pecan		
	rap				
	cap				
	ape				

SORT

c   p   r   an   ap   ape   ace*

TRANSFER

scan   nap   scrape   place

LESSON 92

LETTERS

e e n p r s s t

MAKE

pen	seen	steps*/	preset*	present	presents
pet	sent	pests	resent*		
set	rent	press*			
see	rest	rents			
	pest/				
	step*				

SORT

p   pr   r   s   ent   est

TRANSFER

vent   spent   west   crest

LETTERS

e e l p r s t z

MAKE

see	pets/	peels/	preset*/	pretzels
set	pest	sleep	pester	
pet	rest	sleet*		
	reel	steep*		
	peel	reset*		

SORT

p   r   pr   sl   et   est   eel   eep

TRANSFER

net   vest   steel   creep

LETTERS

e i c n p r

This is a wonderful word for a fairy tale that has a prince in it!

MAKE

in	pin	rice	nicer	prince
	pen	ripe*/	ripen*	
	pie	pier*	price	
	ice	pine*		
	rip	nice		

SORT

p   r   pr   in   ice

TRANSFER

spin   twin   slice   twice

LETTERS

e u d d l p s

MAKE

up	use/	sled	pulse*	puddle	puddles
us	Sue	sped			
	due	dues*/			
	led	used*			
		plus			

SORT

p   s   s (plural)   ue   us   ed

TRANSFER

bus   clue   fled   beds

LESSON 96

LETTERS

e u l l p s y

MAKE

up	use/	sell	pulse	pulley	pulleys
us	sue	yell	spell		
	yes	yelp	yells		
	spy	pull			
	sly	plus			

SORT

p   s   sp   s (plural)   ell   us   y

TRANSFER

fell   bells   bus   sky

142

LETTERS

e i u p p s

MAKE

is	pup	pies	pipes	puppies
us	pep	pipe		
up	sip	pups		
	Sue/			
	use			
	pie			

SORT

p   s   s (plural)   up

TRANSFER

sips   cup   cups

LETTERS

i u l q s t

MAKE

is	lit	slit/	quits	quilts
it	sit/	list	quilt	
	its	suit		
		quit		

SORT

l   qu   s (plural)   it

TRANSFER

fit   spit   split   hits

LESSON 99

LETTERS

a o o c c n r

MAKE

on	can	corn	acorn	raccoon
an	ran		cocoa	
	Ron		croon	
	car/			
	arc			
	oar			

SORT

r   c   an   on   orn   (Name)

TRANSFER

Don   born   morn   clan

145

LETTERS

a a i o d l r r

MAKE

as	our*	rail	radar*	radial*	railroad
or	rod	raid	radio*		
	rid	road			
	lid	roar			
	aid*	lord*			
	ail	load			

SORT

r   l   id   ail   (compound word)

TRANSFER

slid   skid   pail   snail

146

LETTERS

a i o b n r w

MAKE

on	ran	warn	brain	rainbow
an	row	worn*	brown	
	bow	born*	robin*	
	air	barn		
	war	rain		

SORT

b br w an orn* ain

(compound word)

TRANSFER

plan torn* scorn* train

LESSON 102

LETTERS

a a i f l l n r

MAKE

in	ran	fair	frail	rainfall
an	fan	fail	frill	
	far	rail	flair	
	fir	rain*	final*	
	air	fall*		

SORT

f   r   fr   an   air   ail

(compound word)

TRANSFER

Fran   chair   snail   trail

LETTERS

a a o m n r

Here is a word to make when reading to your class
any of the *Ramona* books by Beverly Cleary.

MAKE

or	ram/	roam	aroma*	Ramona
on	arm	moan	manor	
an	man	morn*/		
am	ran	norm*		

SORT

m   r   am   an

TRANSFER

van   plan   ham   slam

LETTERS

e e c c l r y

This is an important science word!

MAKE

cry	reel	leery*	celery*	recycle
rye	rely	cycle	cycler	
eye	eery*			
eel				

SORT

r   c   y (two pronunciations)   s (plural)   **eel**

TRANSFER

try   sly   heel   wheel

LETTERS

e e i l p r s t

MAKE

is	sit	pets/	reels*	preset*	replies*	reptiles
it	pit/	pest	repel*	ripest		
	tip	rest	reset			
	rip	ripe				
	pet	rips				
		reel*				

SORT

r   s   t   s (plural)   it   ip   est

TRANSFER

skit   split   vest   snip

LETTERS

a e d r r s w

(two secret words)

MAKE

Ed	red	draw	draws	reward/	drawers/
	ear	dear/		drawer	rewards
	was/	read			
	saw	rear			
	raw				

SORT

d   r   dr   w   ed   aw   ear

TRANSFER

jaw   slaw   fled   hear

LETTERS

o u d h l p r

MAKE

do	hop	hour*	proud*	uphold/	Rudolph
up	rod	lord*		holdup	
	old	hold			
	our*	drop			
		loud			

SORT

h   l   r   op   old   our   oud

our-hour*

TRANSFER

flop   mold   scold   scour*

LESSON 108

LETTERS

e e i c c n s

MAKE

is   see   ices   scene   nieces*   science
in   ice   nice   since*   scenic*
    seen   niece*

SORT

s   sc   s (plural)   in   ice
seen-scene

TRANSFER

pin   skin   dice   slice

LETTERS

a e o n s s s

This is a good word to make when learning about the seasons!

MAKE

as	son	seas	noses	season	seasons
an	one	sons			
on/	sea	ones/			
no		nose			
so					

SORT

s   n   s (plural)   o

nos-nose

TRANSFER

go   yo   pro   pros

LETTERS

e e i d g l n s

This is a good word to use at planting time!

MAKE

in	see	legs	slide	seeing	seeding	seedling
is	end/	send	sling*			
	den	slid				
	lid	sing*/				
	leg	sign*				

SORT

s   l   sl   ing (ending)   id   end   ing*

TRANSFER

skid   bend   spend   swing*

LETTERS

a e h p s s

MAKE

as	she	sash*	shape	phases/
he	sea	seas	ashes*	shapes
	pea/	peas	phase	
	ape			
	has*/			
	ash*			

SORT

h   s   ape   ash*   e   ea

TRANSFER

we   drape   lash*   crash*

LETTERS

e i g h l s

This is a winter or winter holiday word.

MAKE

is	she	legs/	sleigh
hi	his	gels	
he	lie	sigh	
	gel/	lies	
	leg		

SORT

g   l   h   s (plural)   e   is

TRANSFER

me   we   sleighs

LETTERS

e l p s t

(two secret words)

Here is another easy lesson!

MAKE

let	pets/	pelts/
set	step	slept
pet	pest/	
	pelt	

SORT

p　　s　　s (plural)　　et

TRANSFER

met　vet　sets　steps

LESSON 114

LETTERS

e i g l l m n s

This is one of your five senses or a science word!

MAKE

me	men	legs	slime/	single*	selling	smelling
see	line	smile	mingle*			
leg	lime/	smell				
	mile	sling*				
	mine*					
	slim					

SORT

m   l   sl   sm   ing (ending)   ile   ime   ine*   ingle*

TRANSFER

dime   crime   whine*   shingle*

LETTERS

a o b l l n s w

MAKE

as	was/	bowl/	balls	sallow*	snowball
	saw	blow	bowls/		
	law	slow	blows		
	low	snow	blown		
	bow	ball			

SORT

b bl s sn s (plural) aw ow

Remember to talk about the two pronunciations and three meanings for the word *bow*.

TRANSFER

jaw claw show crows

L·E·S·S·O·N 116

L·E·T·T·E·R·S

a o m n n s w

This is a favorite word to make during the winter season!

M·A·K·E

so	man	sown*/	woman	snowman
no	Sam	snow		
am	saw	swan		
an	sow	swam		
	won/			
	now/			
	own*			

S·O·R·T

s   sn   sw   am   an   ow   own*

T·R·A·N·S·F·E·R

jam   slow   scan   known*

LETTERS

o n s w y

This is a winter word!

MAKE

no	now/	nosy	snowy
	own/	snow/	
	won	sown/	
	son/	owns	
	nos		

SORT

n   s   sn   s (plural)   y   on   own

TRANSFER

ton   sons   grown   blown

LETTERS

i o g n r s t
(two secret words)

This could be a fall word or a math word!

MAKE

so	rot	tong	sting	string	storing/
to	got	song		strong	sorting
in	not/	sing			
or	ton	ring			

SORT

s   st   r   str   ing (ending)   ot   ong   ing

TRANSFER

plot   wrong   swing   swinging

LETTERS

i g n p r s

Here is a spring word!

MAKE

in   pin   rips   rings   spring
      pig   grip
      sip   grin/
      rip   ring
           sing
           spin

SORT

p   gr   s (plural)   in   ip   ing

TRANSFER

twin   hips   slip   fling

LESSON 120

LETTERS

e i k l n p r s

MAKE

is	pin	snip/	spike	silken*	sprinkle
in	ink	spin	spine*	sinker*	
	ski	skin/	skier*		
	sir*	sink			
	sip	slip			
		skip			

SORT

s   sk   sp   ip   in   ink

TRANSFER

chin   clip   trip   wink

LETTERS

o u p r s t

Here is another wonderful word to make when planting.

MAKE

to	top/	pout	sport*	sprout
	pot	rout	spout	
	rot	stop/	spurt*	
	rut	spot/		
	out	tops/		
		post		
		port*		

SORT

p   t   r   op   ot   out   ort

TRANSFER

drop   hot   shout   fort*

LESSON 122

e i o r s s t

This is a good word to make on any day you read a story.

MAKE

is	sit	tore	store	stores/	stories
it	sir	sore		sorest*	
	set	sort*		sister*	
	toe	stir			

SORT

s   t   st   s (plural)   it   ir   ore

TRANSFER

fit   fir   more   score

168

LETTERS

o m r s t y

MAKE

or	try	sort	storm	stormy
my	toy	toys	story	
	Roy	Troy		
	Tom	most		
	rot			

SORT

t   m   st   oy   y (two sounds)   (Names)

TRANSFER

boy   joy   sky   fly

LETTERS

aubcrstt

MAKE

us	sat	stub	start	subtract
as	bat/	stab	strut/	
at	tab	star	trust	
	tub	scar		
	sub			

SORT

s t ab at ar ub

TRANSFER

grab scat jar scrub

LETTERS

e u m m r s

Here is a word to make in the summertime!

MAKE

me	use/	sure/	serum*	summer
us	sue	user		
	sum	muse*		
	rum			

SORT

m   s   use   um

TRANSFER

gum   hum   plum   fuse*

LETTERS

i u g h l n s t

Plants need sunlight; make this word when you study plants.

MAKE

is	sit	sung*	sling	slight	sunlight
it	sun	sing	sting	nights	
			stung*	lights	
			sight		
			night		
			light		

SORT

s   sl   st   s (plural)   ing   ight   ung*

(compound word)

TRANSFER

bring   might   flight   stings

LETTERS

e i u h n n s s

MAKE

us	sun	hens	shine	shines	sunshine
in	she	nine	sinus*	wisher*	
	his	shin*			
	hen				

SORT

h   s   sh   s (plural)   in   ine

TRANSFER

skin   spin   spine   vines

LESSON 128

LETTERS

a e b l t

MAKE

at	bat/	late/	table
	tab	tale/	
	lab	teal	
	let	belt	
	bet	beat	
	tea/	able	
	eat/		
	ate		

SORT

b   l   t   ab   at   ate   eat   able

TRANSFER

cab   plate   wheat   cable

LETTERS

a o c s t

This is a good word to make during a foods or Mexican theme!

MAKE

as	sat	coat	coats/
at	cat/	cost	coast/
	act	cast/	tacos
	oat	cats/	
	cot	scat	
		oats	

SORT

c   s (plural)   at   oat

TRANSFER

flat   splat   float   goats

LETTERS

a e e r s t

MAKE

as	sat	seat/	trees	eaters/
at	set	east	tears*	teaser*
	see	ears	tease*	
	sea	star	tears	
	eat	tear*	reset*	
		tree	eater	

SORT

s   t   tr   ee   eat

sea-see

Help the children understand the two pronunciations and meanings for the word *tear*.

TRANSFER

wheat   pleat   knee   treat

LETTERS

e e i b l r r t

Here is a word to make when you read about someone
having a terrible day!

MAKE

it	bit	tire	tribe/	retire	terrible
	bet	tile	biter		
	let	bite			
	lie	belt			
	tie				

SORT

b   t   et   ie

TRANSFER

net   vet   die   pie

LETTERS

u c k r s t

(two secret words)

MAKE

us	rut	cuts	truck	struck/
	cut	ruts/	tucks	trucks
		rust	stuck	
		suck	crust	
		tuck		

SORT

c   r   t   s (plural)   ut   uck   ust

TRANSFER

nut   strut   luck   trust

LETTERS

e u k r s t y

This lesson could follow the story
One Tough Turkey by Steven Kroll or could be used during November.

MAKE

us	use/	ruts/	rusty	turkey	turkeys
	Sue	rust			
	yes	rest			
	yet	true			
	sky	keys			
	try				
	rut				

SORT

r   y   tr   s (plural)   y   ue

TRANSFER

blue   glue   dry   fly

179

LESSON 134

a e u b l l m r

MAKE

am	ram/	ball	bluer	rumble*	umbrella
	arm	bell	blame	ramble*	
	rub	bull	mural*	lumber	
	bar	blue		marble*	
	ear	dear			
	all	mule*			
		lame			

SORT

b   bl   m   am   ame   all   ear

TRANSFER

slam   stall   smear   tame

LETTERS

a e e i l n n t v

Here is a February word!

MAKE

it	van	late	event*	valentine
at	tan/	lane	eaten*	
an	ant	line	leave	
	let	vine		
	ate	even*		

SORT

v   l   an   ate   ine

TRANSFER

plan   skate   shine   spine

LESSON 136

LETTERS

a e i g n r t w

MAKE

at   ant/   want   water   waiter*   wearing   watering
an   tan   went   write   writer   tearing
      ate*/ wait* twine*
      eat   wear   anger*
      ear   tear

SORT

w   wr   er* (ending)   ing (ending)   an

TRANSFER

van   plan   wanting   waiting

L·E·T·T·E·R·S

a e e h r t w

Make this word during a weather theme!

M·A·K·E

at	rat	heat	three/	heater*	weather
	ear	hear	there		
	eat	here	where		
		wear	wheat		
		tear*	eater*		
		tree			
		tear			

S·O·R·T

h   th   w   wh   er (ending)   at   ear   eat

here-hear   wear-where

Help your students understand the two pronunciations and meanings for the word *tear*.

T·R·A·N·S·F·E·R

that   near   meat   beat

LETTERS

a e h l s w

MAKE

as	has/	seal*/	heals/	whales
	ash	sale	leash	
	was/	slaw/	whale	
	saw	laws		
	law	wash		
	sea	heal		

SORT

s   l   s (plural)   aw   ale

TRANSFER

claw   draw   scale   scales

LETTERS

e i h p r s w

MAKE

is	his	ship	wiser	wipers	whisper
	hip	whip	wiper	wisher	
	rip	wish	swipe		
	sip	wipe			
	sir	wise			

SORT

h s w wh ip ipe

TRANSFER

slip clip pipe ripe

LETTERS

i i u c c h n z

MAKE

hi   inch/   cinch   zucchini
in   chin
chic
zinc

SORT

ch   z   in   inch

TRANSFER

win   spin   pinch   finch

PATTERNS INDEX

Note: Warm-up lesson words are indicated by a numeral in parentheses following the word. For example, spend (#4).

■ Prefixes, Suffixes, and Parts of Words ■

de	detective
ed	Dancer friendly Madeline
er	feeders gardens matter summer watering weather
ing	camping counting graphing glowing growing magnetic planting playing seedling smelling sorting watering
ly	friendly
s, es	acorns artists castles contest crowds discover feeders fingers flames fruits gardens ghosts giants grapes guitars Indians jackets leaves letters longest machines mammals manners measure parties pasta patterns penguins Pilgrims puddles pulleys puppies quilts recycle reptiles science seasons sleigh slept snowball snowy spring stories sunlight sunshine tacos turkeys trucks whales
un	nuclear
y (rainy)	holidays snowy stormy

■ Consonants, Blends, and Digraphs ■

b	alphabet bathroom beavers bedroom birthday bunnies buttons horrible rainbow snowball table terrible umbrella
bl	snowball umbrella
br	birthday rainbow
c (cat, city)	acorns camping castle claps (#1) Clifford clowns contest Corduroy counting crowds curtain Dancer decorate fiction forecast jackets macaroni nuclear overcast Prancer raccoon recycle tacos trucks

ch	cheering machines zucchini
cl	clowns duckling nuclear
cr	crowds
d	adding bedroom Dancer dents (#3) decorate detective discover duckling holidays kingdom rewards spend (#4)
dr	discover dragon rewards
f	Clifford family feeders fiction fingers forecast friendly frogs (#7) fruits rainfall
fl	flames friendly
fr	friendly rainfall
g (girl, gym)	gardens geometry ghosts giants glowing grapes graphing growing longest Pilgrims sleigh stung (#9)
gl	glowing
gr	fingers gardens graphing growing spring
h	alphabet Anthony author birthday cheering chicken Dasher Earth ghosts Harold heart hints (#5) holidays horrible hundreds hunts (#10) machines Rudolph shapes sleigh sunshine weather whisper
j	jackets
k	chicken kingdom knocking
kn (know)	knocking
l	duckling electric glowing Harold holidays journal leaves Madeline nuclear playing quilts railroad Rudolph seedling sleigh smelling table valentine whales
m	autumn camping family geometry macaroni machines Madeline magnetic mammals manners matter measure ornament Ramona smelling stormy summer umbrella
n	chicken contest dents (#3) longest Madeline manners nature ornament seasons snowy
p	airplane escape grapes graphing painter parties patterns penguins Pilgrims piñata

	planting playing practice Prancer presents pretzels prince puddles pulleys puppies slept spend (#4) sport (#8) spring sprout
pl	airplane planting playing
pr	practice presents pretzels prince
qu	quilts
r	airplane bathroom bedroom birthday cheering Corduroy crowds curtain Dancer Dasher decorate dinosaur dragons Earth gardens grapes graphing growing guitars heart horrible hundreds journal kangaroo letters macaroni nature orange overcast parties Pilgrims practice Prancer presents pretzels prince raccoons railroad rainfall Ramona recycle reptiles rewards Rudolph sorting sprout trucks turkeys
s	artists bunnies castle claps (#1) dinosaur discover dragons escape feeders fingers flames fruits giants hints (#5) hunts (#10) Indians jackets leaves letters mammals measure pasta patterns penguins Pilgrims presents puddles pulleys puppies reptiles science seasons seedling shapes slept snowball snowman snowy sorting spend (#4) split (#6) sport (#8) sprinkle stand (#2) stories stung (#9) subtract summer sunlight sunshine teaser whales whisper
sc	acorns castle science
sh	Dasher sunshine
sk	sprinkle
sl	pretzels seedling smelling sunlight
sm	smelling
sn	snowball snowman snowy
sp	pasta pulleys sprinkle
st	artists guitars jackets stories stormy sunlight
str	sorting
sw	snowman

t	Anthony artists author autumn counting curtains decorate detectives electric fiction geometry giants guitars longest matter pasta piñata planting reptiles sprout stories stormy subtract table teaser terrible trucks
th	weather
tr	geometry teaser turkeys
v	beavers overcast valentine
w	crowds glowing growing rainbow rewards watering weather
wh	weather whisper
wr	watering
y	pulleys turkeys
z	zucchini

■ Homophones ■

ad-add	adding
bear-bare	beavers
dear-deer	decorate
hear-here	weather
herd-heard	Dasher
in-inn	Indians knocking
hour-our	author Rudolph
made-maid	Madeline
nos-nose	seasons
ring-wring	growing
sea-see	escape leaves measure teaser
seam-seem	measure
seen-scene	science
tide-tied	detective
wear-where	weather

■ Phonograms, Rhymes, and Chunks ■

ab	subtract table
able	table
ace	escape Prancer

190

ack*	jackets
act	practice
ad	adding Dasher Harold
ag	dragons gardens giants kangaroo orange
age	grapes orange
aid	birthday Madeline
ail	airplane family Madeline planting railroad rainfall
ain*	airplane camping curtain giants graphing macaroni machines painter planting playing rainbow
air	rainfall
aise	parties
ake*	jackets
al	claps (#1) mammal
ale*	castle whales
all*	umbrella
am	autumn macaroni machines mammals matter ornament Ramona snowman umbrella
ame*	flames magnetic manners umbrella
an*	acorns airplane Anthony autumn camping Dancer Indians journal kangaroo macaroni machines Madeline magnetic manners nature orange planting playing Prancer raccoon rainbow rainfall Ramona snowman stand (#2) valentine watering
and	dragons Indians Madeline stand (#2)
ang	dragons
ant	piñata
ap*	camping claps (#1) grapes graphing pasta Prancer
ape	escape Prancer shape
ar	guitars subtract
art	artists painter practice
ase	beavers
ash*	Dasher holidays shapes

ask	jackets
at*	alphabet Anthony artists author autumn bathroom castle guitar heart magnetic nature overcast painter parties pasta patterns piñata practice subtract table tacos weather
ate*	alphabet decorate Earth forecast heart least overcast table valentine
ave	beavers leaves
aw*	rewards snowball whales
ay*	birthday family holidays playing
e (he)	flames shapes sleigh
ea	escape
eal	flames
ean	nuclear
ear	Dasher Dancer decorate gardens heart manners measure nature nuclear orange ornament rewards umbrella weather
eat*	castle Earth forecast heart magnetic matter nature ornament table teaser weather
eck	chicken
ed	bedroom feeders hundreds puddles rewards spend (#4)
ee	leaves
eel	pretzels recycle
eep	pretzels
eet	geometry letters
et	alphabet castle painter pretzels slept
elf	flames
ell*	pulleys
en	chicken dents (#3) hundreds spend (#4)
end	friendly hundreds Madeline seedling spend (#4)
ent	dents (#3) contest presents
erm	geometry

est*	contest letters overcast parties presents pretzels reptiles
et	alphabet castle dents (#3) painter patterns pretzels slept
ice*	cheering detective discover electric practice prince science
ick*	chicken knocking
id	birthday duckling railroad seedling
ie (tie)	detective electric terrible
ig	Pilgrims
ight*	sunlight
ile	smelling
ime	smelling
in*	airplane bunnies chicken duckling finger fiction friendly giants glowing graphing growing hints (#5) kingdom knocking machines penguins piñata playing prince science spring sprinkle sunshine zucchini
inch	zucchini
ind	kingdom
ine*	friendly penguins smelling sunshine valentine
ing*	duckling fingers growing kingdom seedling spring sunlight
ingle	smelling
ink*	duckling knocking sprinkle
ip*	parties Pilgrims reptiles split (#6) spring sprinkle whisper
ipe	whisper
ir	artists fingers fruits stories
is	sleigh
it*	electric fruits giants guitars hints (#5) piñata split (#6) stories practice quilts reptiles sport (#8)
ive	discover
o (no)	frogs (#7) seasons sport (#8)

oad	Harold
oar	dinosaur
oat	tacos
od	Corduroy crowds
og	frogs (#7)
oil	Clifford horrible
old	Clifford Harold holidays Rudolph
ole	horrible
on	journal kangaroo raccoon snowy
one	longest
ong	sorting
oom	bathroom bedroom
oat	bathroom
op*	Rudolph sprout
or	frogs (#7) journal
ore*	bedroom stories
ord	Clifford
orn	acorns raccoon rainbow
ort	sprout
ost	ghost
ot*	Anthony contest counting fiction ghosts longest sorting sport (#8) sprout
oud	Rudolph
ound	dinosaur
our	author dinosaur Rudolph
out	author buttons sprout
ow (cow, low)	clowns crowds glowing growing snowball snowman
own	snowman snowy
oy	Corduroy geometry stormy
ub	bunnies subtract
uck*	duckling trucks
ue	puddles turkeys
ug*	guitars stung (#9)

um	summer
un	curtain dinosaurs hunts (#10) stung (#9)
ung	sunlight
up	puppies
urf	fruits
us	bunnies buttons puddles pulleys stung (#9)
use	summer
ust	trucks
ut	buttons curtain hunts (#10) trucks stung (#9)
y (fly, fishy)	Corduroy family holidays pulleys recycle snowy stormy turkeys

■ Compound Words ■

airman	*from*	macaroni
airplane	*from*	airplane
overcast	*from*	overcast
railroad	*from*	railroad
rainbow	*from*	rainbow
rainfall	*from*	rainfall
snowball	*from*	snowball
snowman	*from*	snowman
sunlight	*from*	sunlight

Dear **FAMILIES**,

Making More Words is an important activity that we work on in class. As we "make words," your child learns more phonics and spelling. As children manipulate the given letters, they discover letter-sound relationships, and as they look for patterns in words, they see how these letter-sound relationships work in words. These two activities help children read and spell even more words! Children enjoy these lessons, but more importantly these skills increase their word knowledge, which will help them become even better students and readers.

When your child brings home a Take-Home Sheet containing brief instructions, a strip of letters, and 12 empty word boxes, have him or her cut the letterstrip apart into the individual letters. (Leave the word boxes uncut for the moment.) Next, work together with your child to make as many words as you can, or let your child see how many words he or she can make unaided. As the words are made, let your child write them in the empty boxes. Finally, have your child cut the word boxes apart, and take some of the words and put them into groups (your child knows what to do).

Have fun working together "making more words"!

Sincerely,

_____

Your Child's Teacher

196

TAKE-HOME SHEET

Making More Words

The letters needed to "make more words" tonight are at the top of the form below. To begin, have your child cut the letters apart; then work together to see how many words you can make. As you make a word, let your child write the words in one of the empty boxes below. To finish, ask your child to cut the words out and sort or group them by beginning or ending sounds or spelling patterns.

LETTER CARD REPRODUCIBLES

Patterns to create letter cards for student use are found on pages 199–204. The letters can be reproduced with the lowercase letters on one side of a page and the uppercase letters on the other side, so that the two pages to be run back-to-back are reversed. You may prefer to reproduce the upper- and lowercase letters on separate sheets of paper, letting students choose themselves between the two letter forms.

The vowel patterns are found on pages 199–200. Print or photocopy the vowels on colored index cards or cardstock making a complete set for each child in your class.

The consonant patterns are found on pages 201–204. Reproduce on white index cards or cardstock a complete set of the consonant letters for each student.

Blank letter card forms are provided on pages 205–206. Photocopy the forms, then use them to create your own custom assortment of letters. Reproduce the letters as needed for students to use.

a	a	a	y
e	e	e	y
i	i	i	y
o	o	o	
u	u	u	

Y	A	A	A
Y	E	E	E
Y	I	I	I
	O	O	O
	U	U	U

b	d	h	l
b	f	h	l
c	f	j	m
c	g	j	m
d	g	k	n

L	H	D	B
M	H	F	B
M	J	F	C
M	J	G	C
N	K	G	D

n	q	t	w
n	r	t	x
p	r	v	x
p	s	v	z
q	s	w	z

W	T	Q	N
X	T	R	N
X	V	R	P
Z	V	S	P
Z	W	S	Q